Goodbye, Things

Fumio Sasaki

Maximalist

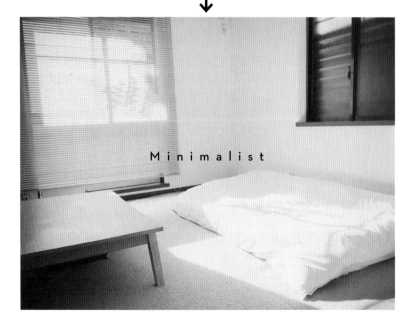

Minimalist

BECOMING MINIMALIST

Both of the pictures on the opposite page are of my old apartment. I couldn't throw things away. As you can see, my possessions kept piling up. I lived in this apartment for ten years, and during that time, it seemed like my life had stopped moving forward. That was when I came across the concept of minimalism—of reducing your belongings to just the minimal essentials. I went from messy maximalism to life as a minimalist. I said goodbye to almost all my things and to my surprise I found I had also changed myself in the process.

HOW I BECAME A MINIMALIST

1. Little by little, using techniques I'll cover in chapter 3, I turned that messy room into a tidy apartment.

2. I got rid of all my books, and even my desk and chair. We call this "simple" living, rather than minimalist living.

3. Finally, I got rid of my mattress, table, and even my TV. I often feel like I'm a Zen monk in training.

Maximalist Life

1. I used to leave my clothes lying around, which resulted in what you might call a peculiar art-installation feel.

2. I drank beer at my messy table, munched on snacks, and played video games. I gained weight of course. Minimalism helped with that as well!

3. I used to enjoy buying antique cameras and strange lamps at online auctions.

4. My hallway, formerly lined with bookshelves. I collected as many CDs and DVDs as I could, but in the end I didn't really cherish any of them.

CASE 1
FUMIO SASAKI

MODEL APARTMENT FOR A MINIMALIST

When I moved out of my old apartment, I chose a simple twenty-square-meter studio with a kitchen. I'm trying to leave it in its clean state, a model apartment for single minimalist living.

This is what the place looks like when I sleep. I use an "airy mattress" from Iris Ohyama, a must-have for Japanese minimalists. Sunlight pours in through the windows, which makes waking up something to look forward to.

Even though I sometimes cook my own meals, my tableware is kept to a minimum. The designs are also minimalist, and cleanup is quick and easy.

Here's a look in my closet, from a down jacket to a suit, some white shirts, and the few pairs of pants that match in a simple style. I'm aiming to create my own uniform with a signature style like Steve Jobs had.

I don't keep a utility rack in my bathroom. I use liquid soap to wash my body and my hair, and after I get out of the bath, I wipe my whole body with a small hand towel.

I keep my apartment and bicycle keys hooked to a thin wallet from abrAsus. I just put this wallet and my iPhone in my pocket and head out whenever and wherever the mood strikes.

THE APARTMENT OF A TRAILBLAZER

Hiji is one of the first people who helped spread the minimalist movement in Japan. His simple Zen-like apartment is home to some of the latest gadgets.

PROFILE

Hiji currently works as a securities dealer. A fan of graphic novels and the pop group Momoiro Clover Z, Hiji was one of the first minimalist bloggers in Japan. Blog: *Mono o motanai minimarisuto* (A minimalist who doesn't own things) at minimarisuto.jp.

Hiji is a hardcore minimalist who leaves nothing lying around. The kitchen has just a refrigerator, rice cooker, and microwave oven.

The "airy mattress" became a necessity for minimalists after Hiji first mentioned it. Fold it up and place the pillow on top to make a "mattress sofa."

Because he has nothing that takes up floor space, there's plenty of room for Hiji to enjoy board games with friends. Carcasonne is one of his favorites.

Is this a sparse closet or what? Pull out a Microsoft Surface Pro and folding chair, and it instantly turns into an office.

Hiji is seen here wearing a Sony head-mounted viewer. He got rid of his TV but can still watch his favorite shows—horror films are especially frightening when you watch them this way.

A MINIMALIST COUPLE LIVING IN COMFORT

Ofumi and her husband threw away a hundred and thirty kilograms' worth of possessions when they moved from a seventy-eight-square meter apartment to a forty-four-square meter apartment. They continue to enjoy their favorite belongings while maintaining a minimalist way of life.

PROFILE

Ofumi and Tee say they were awakened to minimalism just as they were about to build a house. They both have their own blogs: *Minimarisuto-biyori* (A fine day for a minimalist) at mount-hayashi .hatenablog.com, and *Okurete kita minimarisuto* (The belated minimalist) at minimaltee.hateblo.jp. Ofumi is also on Instagram at @ofumi_3.

A handmade hanging scroll from SOU SOU adds flavor to this spare Japanese-style tatami mat room. The couple says it adds a sense of ownership to their rental.

Ofumi keeps an illustrated diary in her Hobonichi Techo planner and shares it on her blog. It's fun just to look at the colors and intricate composition.

While presents received from friends are kept minimal, they are displayed with care. A fine balance is kept between being too sparse and too busy.

The living room wall is decorated with a hand towel from Mina Perhonen and a simple wall clock. It's cute and yet creates a Zen garden–like sense of space.

CASE 4
YAMASAN

MINIMALIST FAMILY LIFE

Yamasan's home is an example of how a family of four can live simply. It's clean throughout and an ideal home for relaxing.

PROFILE

Yamasan is a minimalist supermom who lives with her husband and two kids. She enjoys DIY projects and aims for a beautiful and relaxing atmosphere in her home. Her blog, *Sukunai monode sukkiri kurasu* (Living simply with few things), can be seen at yamasan0521.hatenablog.com.

Yamasan keeps the backyard simple. The ash trees add privacy, and the wooden fence was built by Yamasan herself.

The area that was previously the family "library" has been emptied out, and can now be used as a multi-function room.

The living area, where the family gets together, is the heart of Yamasan's home. As part of her "color minimalism," she only uses hues that are easy on the eyes.

Yamasan's summer wardrobe consists of eight items in minimalist colors. She savors the time she takes to carefully iron them.

The Japanese tatami room serves as a bedroom. Everything in the closet is white so that it's not distracting even when opened up.

CASE 5
KOUTA ITOU

A MINIMALIST GLOBETROTTER

These are the items that Kouta Itou has carefully chosen through trial and error over a period of four years. As long as he has these items, he can travel around the world with no problem. One backpack is all he needs to live.

PROFILE
Kouta is a young minimalist adventurer who travels the globe with his trusted MacBook Pro and creates music wherever he goes. His complete list of belongings can be found on his blog: *Minimalist Music Producer* at minimalist-music-producer.com.

Yamasan keeps the backyard simple. The ash trees add privacy, and the wooden fence was built by Yamasan herself.

The area that was previously the family "library" has been emptied out, and can now be used as a multifunction room.

The living area, where the family gets together, is the heart of Yamasan's home. As part of her "color minimalism," she only uses hues that are easy on the eyes.

Yamasan's summer wardrobe consists of eight items in minimalist colors. She savors the time she takes to carefully iron them.

The Japanese tatami room serves as a bedroom. Everything in the closet is white so that it's not distracting even when opened up.

A MINIMALIST GLOBETROTTER

These are the items that Kouta Itou has carefully chosen through trial and error over a period of four years. As long as he has these items, he can travel around the world with no problem. One backpack is all he needs to live.

PROFILE

Kouta is a young minimalist adventurer who travels the globe with his trusted MacBook Pro and creates music wherever he goes. His complete list of belongings can be found on his blog: *Minimalist Music Producer* at minimalist-music-producer.com.

1. MACBOOK PRO
Kouta can create music wherever he is with with his MacBook Pro.

2. SAWYER MINI
A portable, high-quality water filtration system that removes harmful bacteria, in case you have to drink water that might not be clean.

3. TRAIL WALLET FROM GRANITE GEAR
A durable and lightweight wallet that can be used to store valuables.

4. MONTBELL SLEEPING BAG
A Down Hugger 800 #3 model sleeping bag for cold weather when it isn't possible to sleep in a hammock.

5. HENNESSY HAMMOCK
A nifty tent-and-hammock-in-one that provides a place to sleep as long as there's a place to hang it.

6. BLACK DIAMOND HEADLAMP
This headlamp works as a bright flashlight or even as a lamp in any room.

7. SPIBELT BASIC
A belt worn wrapped around the body that stretches any way you do, so you can always have your valuables on your person.

8. SONY MDR-1ADAC
For true audiophiles, these headphones are compatible with high-resolution audio, and can receive digital data signals.

9. IPHONE AND LOKSAK
The multifunctional iPhone is indispensable. Stored in a LOKSAK case, it's waterproof to sixty meters and can be taken anywhere you go.

10. SONY ALPHA NEX-5N
A digital SLR from Sony. Kouta uses it with a Sigma 30 mm/F2.8 DN lens.

11. AMAZON KINDLE
Kouta's chosen e-reader for travel-friendly reading.

12. SHEMAGH (ARABIAN SCARF)
The versatile *shemagh* can serve as a scarf, mask, hat, towel, or even water filter.

13. CLOTHESLINE ROPE

A convenient rope from Sea to Summit that is compact and designed so your clothes won't slip off.

14. PASSPORT

Kouta keeps this with him at all times in his LOKSAK along with his emergency money.

15. PRECOOKED FOOD PACKS

Kouta's favorite *Donbei* noodles are the kind that come in a pouch so no extra garbage is produced.

16. MULTI-TOOL FROM LEATHERMAN

Kouta uses the Leatherman Squirt PS4 model, which offers an array of tools such as scissors, knives, and a nail file.

17. POWER CABLES AND BATTERY CHARGERS

Kouta uses a silnylon pack from Eagle Creek to gather all the cables for his digital gadgets.

18. EMERGENCY BLANKET

A blanket that can be used in an emergency or when Kouta is just cold. Made by SOL, it's smooth and doesn't feel coarse.

19. BOSE SOUNDLINK MINI

This Bluetooth speaker is essential for Kouta, and offers better sound quality than most high-grade stereo systems.

20. PLUG ADAPTER

A necessity when traveling abroad. Kouta uses an adapter from Muji for its minimal design.

21. MOLESKINE NOTEBOOK

Kouta uses this notebook as a diary and collects messages from the various people he meets during his travels.

22. MOLDEX EARPLUGS

These earplugs keep all kinds of noises minimal. The Goin' Green model offers the best level of protection.

23. POCKET SOAP

Sea to Summit Pocket Soap contains single-use soap leaves, making it easy to do your laundry on the road.

24. TRAVEL KIT

Kouta stores personal grooming items, a lighter, a radio, and other small items in this travel kit.

About the structure of this book

Chapter 1 takes a look at the definition of a minimalist and what exactly it means to be one. It also explores some of the reasons why I believe the minimalist population has been growing in recent years. Chapter 2 asks why we have accumulated so much in the first place. It considers the habits and the desires that we have as humans and the meanings that exist behind all the objects we have. Chapter 3 offers some basic rules and techniques for reducing our material possessions. I've compiled methods for discarding various things, along with an additional list for minimalists who want to part with more items, and also a remedy for minimalists who get addicted to throwing things away. Chapter 4 talks about the changes that I went through when I decreased the number of my possessions to an absolute minimum. Along with the psychological results, it offers a look at the positive things that have happened to me by going minimalist and the sense of happiness that I have become more aware of. Chapter 5 offers more insight into why the changes that I went through have made me happy, and covers more generally what I learned about happiness along the way.

I hope you'll start at the beginning of this book to give you a better sense of minimalism, but it's also okay to read the chapters randomly if you prefer. I think a quick look at chapter 3 will come in handy for anyone who's thinking about reducing the amount of possessions that they now have.

In this book, I've defined minimalism as (1) reducing our necessary items to a minimum, and (2) doing away with excess so we can focus on the things that are truly important to us. People who live that way are the ones I consider to be minimalists.

Goodbye, Things

The New Japanese Minimalism

Fumio Sasaki

Translated by Eriko Sugita

W.W. NORTON & COMPANY
Independent Publishers Since 1923
New York | London

BOKUTACHINI, MOU MONO WA HITSUYOU NAI
Copyright © 2017, 2015 by Fumio Sasaki
English translation rights arranged with WANI BOOKS CO., LTD. through Japan
UNI Agency, Inc., Tokyo, and Gudovitz & Company Literary Agency

Cover design: Chin-Yee Lai
Cover photographs: (teacup) Cathy Pyle / Moment / Getty Images;
(shelf) Matthieu Spohn / PhotoAlto Agency / Getty Images

For information about permission to reproduce selections from this book,
write to Permissions, W. W. Norton & Company, Inc.,
500 Fifth Avenue, New York, NY 10110

For information about special discounts for bulk purchases, please contact
W. W. Norton Special Sales at specialsales@wwnorton.com or 800-233-4830

Manufacturing by Berryville Graphics
Book design by Ellen Cipriano Design
Production manager: Julia Druskin

Library of Congress Cataloging-in-Publication Data
Names: Sasaki, Fumio, 1979–
Title: Goodbye, things : the new Japanese minimalism / Fumio Sasaki ;
translated by Eriko Sugita.
Other titles: Bokutachi ni mō mono wa hitsuyō nai. English
Description: New York : W.W. Norton & Company, 2017.
Identifiers: LCCN 2017002330 | ISBN 9780393609035 (hardcover)
Subjects: LCSH: Simplicity. | Orderliness. | Self-actualization (Psychology) |
Consumption (Economics)—Psychological aspects.
Classification: LCC BJ1496 .S25713 2017 | DDC 179/.9—dc23
LC record available at https://lccn.loc.gov/2017002330

W. W. Norton & Company, Inc.,
500 Fifth Avenue, New York, N.Y. 10110
www.wwnorton.com

W. W. Norton & Company Ltd.,
15 Carlisle Street, London W1D 3BS

5   6   7   8   9   0

Contents

INTRODUCTION   23

1. Why minimalism?   31

2. Why did we accumulate so much
in the first place?   55

3. 55 tips to help you say goodbye to
your things   79

15 more tips for the next stage of your
minimalist journey   137

4. 12 ways I've changed since I said goodbye
to my things   155

5. "Feeling" happy instead of "becoming" happy   245

AFTERWORD AND MAXIMUM THANKS   255

RECAP: FUMIO SASAKI'S MINIMALIST TIPS   261

Introduction

There's happiness in having less. That's why it's time to say good-bye to all our extra things.

That's the minimal version of the message that I'd like to convey in this book. I want to show you how amazing it is to have less, even though that's the complete opposite of how we've been taught to be happy. We think that the more we have, the happier we will be. We never know what tomorrow might bring, so we collect and save as much as we can.

This means we need a lot of money, so we gradually start judging people by how much money they have. We start to realize that money solves most of our problems. You can even change people's minds if the price is right. And if you can buy people's minds, then surely you can buy happiness. So, you convince yourself that you need to make a lot of money so you don't miss out on success. And for you to make money, you need everyone else to spend their money. And so it goes.

Let me tell you a bit about myself. I'm thirty-five years old, male, single, never been married. I work as an editor at a publishing company. I recently moved from the Nakameguro neighborhood in Tokyo, where I lived for a decade, to a neighborhood called Fudomae in a different part of town. The rent is 67,000 yen (about $650) per month (20,000 yen [about $200] less than my last apartment), but the move pretty much wiped out my savings.

Some of you may think that I'm a loser: an unmarried adult with not much money to speak of. The old me would have been way too embarrassed to admit all this. I was filled with useless pride. But I honestly don't care about things like that anymore. The reason is very simple: I'm perfectly happy just as I am.

Ten years ago, I was eager to get into publishing. I wanted a career in which I could think about big ideas and cultural values instead of always being focused on money and material objects. But that initial enthusiasm gradually faded. The publishing industry was going through a difficult period, and for our company to survive, we needed books that would sell, first and foremost. If we didn't publish commercial books, it would be impossible to publish anything, no matter how culturally or intellectually valuable we thought it was. Faced with the realities of the business world, I grew up quickly. The passion that had been burning inside me when I first joined the company began to cool, and I ultimately gave in to the mind-set that in the end, it's all about money.

But then I got rid of most of my material possessions, and that idea was completely turned upside down.

Minimalism is a lifestyle in which you reduce your possessions to the absolute minimum you need. Living as a minimalist with the bare essentials has not only provided superficial benefits like the pleasure of a tidy room or the simple ease of cleaning, it has also led to a more fundamental shift. It's given me a chance to think about what it really means to be happy.

I said goodbye to a lot of things, many of which I'd had for years. And yet now I live each day with a happier spirit. I feel more content now than I ever have in the past.

We all want to be happy. We all work hard at our jobs, studies, sports, parenting, or hobbies because when you get right down to it, we're all just looking for happiness. The quintessential energy that drives us is the desire to be happy.

I wasn't always a minimalist. I used to buy a lot of things, believing that all those possessions would increase my self-worth and lead to a happier life. As you can see in the pictures of my messy room at the beginning of this book, I loved collecting a lot of useless stuff, and I couldn't throw anything away. I was a natural hoarder of all these knickknacks that I thought made me an interesting person.

At the same time, though, I was always comparing myself with other people who had more or better things, which often made me miserable. I didn't know how to make things better. I couldn't focus on anything, and I was always wasting time. I was even starting to regret taking the job I had wanted so much. Alcohol was my escape, and I didn't treat women fairly. I didn't try to change; I thought this was all just part of who I was, and I deserved to be unhappy.

Here's a description of what my apartment used to be like. My room wasn't horribly messy; I could do enough tidying up if my girlfriend was coming over for the weekend to make it look presentable. I tried to set up a "cool" vibe by arranging displays of my favorite decorative pieces, and the indirect lighting made for an inviting atmosphere. On a usual day, though, there were books stacked everywhere because there wasn't enough room on my bookshelves. Most of them were books I thumbed through once or twice, thinking that I would sit down and read them one of these days when I had the time.

The closet was strictly off-limits to visitors—it was crammed with what used to be my favorite clothes. Every once in a while, I would pull something out and think about wearing it, but I never actually did. Most of those outfits I'd only worn a few times, but they were expensive so I held on to them thinking if I washed and ironed them, maybe I'd start wearing them again.

The room was filled with all the things I'd taken up as hobbies and then gotten tired of. There was a guitar and amplifier for beginners, covered with dust. Conversational English workbooks I'd planned to study once I had more free time on my hands. Even a fabulous antique camera, which I of course had never once put a roll of film in.

Because I lost interest in all these hobbies, there was actually never anything I wanted to do at home. I would watch TV, maybe play a game on my smartphone, or go pick up some booze at the convenience store and drink the night away, even though I knew I needed to stop doing that.

Meanwhile, I kept comparing myself with others. A friend from college lived in a posh condo on newly developed land in Tokyo. It had a glitzy entrance and stylish Scandinavian furniture and tableware in the dining room. When I visited, I found myself calculating his rent in my head as he graciously invited me in. He worked for a big company, earned a good salary, married his gorgeous girlfriend, and they'd had a beautiful baby, all dressed up in fashionable baby wear. We'd been kind of alike back in college. What had happened? How did our lives drift so far apart?

Or I'd see a pristine white Ferrari convertible speeding by, showing off. The car is probably worth twice the value of my apartment. I'd gaze dumbly at the Ferrari as it disappeared from view, one foot on the pedal of my secondhand bicycle that I bought from a friend for 5,000 yen (about $50).

I bought lottery tickets, hoping I could catch up in a flash. I broke up with my girlfriend, telling her I couldn't see a future for us in my sad financial state. All the while, I carefully hid my inferiority complex and acted as though there was nothing wrong with my life. But I was miserable, and I made other people miserable, too.

I'm glad I threw away a lot of my belongings. I started to become a new person.

It may sound like I'm exaggerating. Someone once said to me, "All you did is throw things away," which is true. I haven't accomplished much yet and there's nothing that I can really be proud of, at least not at this point in my life. But one thing I'm sure of is that by having fewer things around, I've started feeling happier each day. I'm slowly beginning to understand what happiness is.

If you are anything like how I used to be—miserable, constantly comparing yourself with others, or just believing your life sucks—I think you should try saying goodbye to some of your things. Yes, there are certainly people who haven't ever been attached to material objects, or those rare geniuses who can thrive amid the chaos of their possessions. But I want to think about the ways that ordinary people like you and me can find the real pleasures in life. Everyone wants to be happy. But trying to buy happiness only makes us happy for a little while. We are lost when it comes to true happiness.

After what I've been through, I think saying goodbye to your things is more than an exercise in tidying up. I think it's an exercise in thinking about true happiness.

Maybe that sounds grandiose. But I seriously think it's true.

We are more interested in making others believe we are happy than in trying to be happy ourselves.

—FRANÇOIS DE LA ROCHEFOUCAULD

You're not your job. You're not how much money you have in the bank. You're not the car you drive. You're not the contents of your wallet. You're not your fucking khakis.

—TYLER DURDEN, *FIGHT CLUB*

Happiness is not having what you want, but wanting what you have.

—RABBI HYMAN SCHACHTEL

1

Why
minimalism?

Everyone started out as a minimalist

When you think about it, there isn't a single person who was born into this world holding some material possession in their hands.

Everyone started out a minimalist. Our worth is not the sum of our belongings. Possessions can make us happy only for brief periods. Unnecessary material objects suck up our time, our energy, and our freedom. I think minimalists are starting to realize that.

Anyone can imagine the invigorating feeling that comes with de-cluttering and minimizing, even if there are mountains of things lying around at home right now. It's because we've all been through something like it at one time or another. Think, for example, of going away on a trip.

Before you head out, you're probably busy packing at the last minute. You go through your checklist of items to take with you and although everything looks fine, you can't help feeling that there's something that you've forgotten. But the clock is ticking, and it's time to go. You give up, get up, lock the door behind you, and start rolling your suitcase along the pavement—with a strange sense of freedom. You think then that yes, you can manage to live for a while with this one suitcase. Maybe you've forgotten to bring something along, but hey, you can always get whatever you need wherever you're going.

You arrive at your destination and lie down on the freshly made bed—or the tatami mat if it happens to be a Japanese-style inn. It feels good. The room is clean and uncluttered. You aren't surrounded by all the things that usually distract you, the stuff that takes up so much of your attention. That's why travel accommodations often feel so comfortable. You set down your bag and step out for a walk around the neighborhood. You feel light on your feet, like you could keep walking forever. You have the freedom to go wherever you want. Time is on your side, and you don't have the usual chores or work responsibilities weighing you down.

This is a minimalist state, and most of us have experienced it at one time or another. The reverse is true, too, however.

Imagine your return flight. Though your belongings were packed neatly in your suitcase before you started your trip, everything has now been squeezed inside in a mess. The souvenirs you bought don't fit in your suitcase, so you're also carrying a couple of big paper bags. The admission tickets and receipts from the tourist sites you visited—you're going to sort through those later, right? That's why they're still stuffed in your pockets. You're standing in the security line and the time has come to pull out your boarding pass. Uh-oh, where have you put it? You start looking everywhere but you can't seem to find it. You're getting closer to the head of the line and your frustration mounts. You can sense the icy glares of the other people who are standing in the long line behind you, like your back is being pierced by pins and needles.

This is a maximalist state. These stressful situations tend to happen when you're saddled with more objects than you can handle. You aren't able to separate out what's really important.

With our desire to have more, we find ourselves spending more and more time and energy to manage and maintain everything we have. We try so hard to do this that the things that were supposed to help us end up ruling us.

Tyler Durden said it best in the film *Fight Club*: "The things you own end up owning you."

A day in my life before I became a minimalist

Back when I used to have a lot of possessions, a typical day in my life used to go like this: I'd come home from work, haphazardly take off my clothes, and leave them lying around wherever I happened to be. Then I'd take a shower, always noticing the crack in the bathroom sink that needed to be repaired. I'd sit in front of the TV to catch up on the shows I'd taped or maybe watch one of the movies I'd rented, and crack open a can of beer. Wine was my drink of choice for later in the evening, and there were times when I'd finish a bottle too quickly and I'd have to dash over to the nearby convenience store, already drunk.

I once heard a line that went *Liquor is not happiness but a temporary respite from unhappiness.* That was exactly the case for me. I wanted to forget about how miserable I was, if only for a brief moment.

I'd get up the next morning feeling cranky and reluctant to get out of bed. I would hit the snooze button on my alarm clock every ten minutes until the sun was high in the sky and it was well past time to get ready for work. I'd feel weary with a throbbing headache from drinking too much yet again. Sitting on the toilet, I'd pinch the fat around my abdomen as I took care of business. Then I'd open the clothes dryer and pull out the crumpled Uniqlo shirt I threw in there last night, put it on with a quick glance at the clothes that had yet to be washed, and step out the door.

I'd make my way to the office, sick and tired of the same old commute. I'd go online and visit an anonymous bulletin board to pass the time since I know I can't concentrate on my work first thing in the morning. Check my e-mail obsessively and respond immediately, thinking that this somehow showed I was great at my job. All the while, I'd keep putting off the actual important work. I'd leave the office at the end of the day, not because I had finished everything that I was supposed to finish but simply because it was time to go home.

Back in my preminimalist days, I was full of excuses. I couldn't get up in the morning because I'd been working late. I'm fat because it's in my genes. I could get right down to work if I had a better living environment. There's no room to put anything away in my home, though, so how can I help it if it happens to be a mess? I only rent it—it isn't like I own it—so what's the use in trying to clean it up? Of course I'd keep it clean if it were a spacious home that I actually owned, but with my limited salary I can't move to a bigger place.

The excuses were endless, the thoughts running through my mind all negative. I was stuck in that mind-set and yet because of my useless sense of pride, I was too afraid of failing to take any action to change things.

A day in my life as a minimalist

Since I minimized my possessions, a drastic change has occurred in my daily life. I come home from work and take a bath. I always leave the tub sparkling clean. I finish my bath and change into a favorite outfit for relaxing at home. Since I got rid of my TV, I read a book or write instead. I no longer drink alone. I go to bed after taking my time doing some stretching exercises, using the space that used to be filled with all my stuff.

I now get up as the sun rises, and I no longer have to rely on my alarm clock. With my material objects gone, the shining rays of the morning sun are reflected against the white wallpaper and brighten up the apartment. The mere act of getting up in the morning, which had been a tough thing for me to do in the past, has now become a pleasant routine. I put away my futon pad. I take time to enjoy my breakfast and savor the espresso I make on my Macchinetta, always cleaning up the breakfast dishes right after my meal. I sit down and meditate to help clear my mind. I vacuum my apartment every day. I do the laundry if the weather is nice. I put on clothes that have been neatly folded and leave the apartment feeling good. I now enjoy taking the same route to work every day—it allows me to appreciate the changes of the four seasons.

I can't believe how my life has changed. I got rid of my possessions, and I'm now truly happy.

The things I threw away

Let me share with you the things that I've thrown away.

- All my books, including my bookshelves. I must have spent at least a million yen (about $10,000) on those books, but I sold them for 20,000 yen (about $200).
- My boom box and all my CDs. I have to admit, I used to pretend to be an expert on various kinds of music, even if they didn't really interest me.
- A big kitchen cupboard that had been fully stocked for some reason, even though I was living alone.
- A collection of antique pieces—which I recklessly bought at a bunch of auctions.
- Expensive clothes that didn't fit, but that I thought I'd wear when I lost weight . . . one of these days.
- A full set of camera equipment. I had even rigged up a darkroom. What was I thinking?
- Various tools for maintaining my bicycle.
- An electric guitar and amplifier, both covered with

dust. They'd been left sitting around because I didn't want to admit to myself that my attempt to become a fantastic musician had failed.

* A desk and a dining table, both far too large for a bachelor. Even though I didn't invite people over, I had this desire to share a simmering hot pot with someone.

* A Tempur-Pedic full-size mattress—extremely comfortable but extremely heavy, too.

* A forty-two-inch TV that was clearly out of place in my one-hundred-square-foot room, but supposedly showed that I was a serious fan of movies.

* A full home theater setup and a PS3.

* Adult videos I had stored on my hard drive. These may have been the items it took me the most courage to part with.

* Roll upon roll of developed photographs, piled up in stacks and stuck together.

* Treasured letters I'd been saving since kindergarten.

Because I had a hard time just discarding things, I took photos of everything that I threw away. I shot pictures of the covers of all my books, too. There must be at least three thousand pictures stored on my hard drive.

Now that I think about it, I had everything I needed: a big TV, a home theater set, a computer, an iPhone, a comfortable bed, and more. But even though I had all of life's necessities, I kept thinking about what was missing in my life.

I could watch movies with my girlfriend in style, if only I had a leather loveseat. (I could casually put my arm around her during the film.) I'd probably look smart if I had a floor-to-ceiling bookshelf. I could invite friends over for parties if I had a grand rooftop terrace. All the apartments I saw featured in magazines had these things, and yet I had none of them. If only I had them, people would start noticing me.

It was all the things I *didn't* have that were standing between me and my happiness. That's the way my mind used to work.

Why I became a minimalist

People become minimalists for different reasons. There are those whose lives spiral out of control because of the effects of their material belongings. There are others who are filthy rich but have remained unhappy no matter how many things they accumulated. Some people get rid of their possessions little by little every time they move. Others part with their things in an attempt to break out of a depression. And there are also others whose way of thinking has changed after experiencing a major natural disaster.

I'm a classic case of the first type. I became a minimalist in reaction to my overly cluttered pigpen. I could never throw things away. I loved all the things I had collected.

Let's say that someone left me a note at the office, telling me that someone had called. The mere thought that the person had taken the time and effort to leave me this note made it impossible to throw it away.

Back when I first came to Tokyo from my hometown in Kagawa Prefecture, my apartment contained nothing but the bare essentials. But because I couldn't throw anything away, it gradually became a palace of clutter. And I could come up with justifications for all of it.

I used to like taking pictures. I wanted to capture precious moments and make them mine. I wanted to hang on to everything that might someday become a fond memory.

The books I read are like a part of me, so naturally, I couldn't part with them, either. I wanted to share my favorite movies and music with others. There were always hobbies I wanted to take up when I had the time.

I couldn't throw away anything expensive. That would be such a waste. And just because I wasn't using something at that moment, it didn't mean I wasn't going to use it someday.

This is just some of the reasoning that went through my head as I kept accumulating things.

It was the complete opposite of how I now feel. I was a maximalist, determined to save everything, to buy the coolest, biggest, heaviest items I could afford.

And as my belongings started to take up more and more room, I began to be overwhelmed by them, spending all my energy on my objects while still hating myself for not being able to make good use of them all. Yet no matter how much I accumulated, my attention was still focused on the things I didn't have. I became jealous of other people. Even then, I couldn't throw anything away, and so I was stuck going around and around in a vicious circle of self-loathing.

But by getting rid of my things, I've finally started to break out of that situation. If you're anything like I was—dissatisfied with your life, insecure, unhappy—try reducing your belongings. You'll start to change.

Unhappiness isn't just the result of genetics or past trauma or career trouble. I think that some of our unhappiness is simply due to the burden of all our things.

The Japanese used to be minimalists

We're all born into this world as minimalists, but we Japanese used to lead minimalist lives as well. Foreigners who came to Japan before our industrialization were shocked. While it might be hard to imagine today, most people owned perhaps two or three kimonos, always kept fresh and clean, as their entire wardrobe. They packed light, their legs were strong, and they could walk wherever they needed to go. Homes were simple structures that could quickly be rebuilt, and people didn't tend to live in the same place all their lives. Japanese culture used to be a minimalist culture.

Let's look at the Japanese tea ceremony as an example. There's nothing excessive about a tea ceremony room. It has a tiny door that serves as an entrance, and it's impossible to walk through it if you have your chest puffed out with self-importance. Even samurai warriors of bygone days had not been not allowed to take a sword inside a tea ceremony room. It didn't and still doesn't matter today who you are—whether you're a VIP or rich or poor, this is simply a room for people to savor the taste of a cup of tea and share thoughts about one another.

Minimalism imported back to Japan

The American company Apple has an intriguing connection to the minimalist culture of Japan. Many minimalists are fond of Apple products and of Apple's founder, Steve Jobs.

The products that Jobs created always avoided excess. The iPhone only has one button, and you don't have to worry about being stuck with a lot of extra wires and ports when you buy a Mac. Apple products generally don't include operating manuals. I think this is all due to the fact that Jobs had been a minimalist, and he was known to be a believer in Japanese Zen, which teaches minimalism.

It's quite well-known that Steve Jobs considered Master Kobun Otogawa of the Soto school his master and had at one point seriously considered studying Zen at the temple Eiheiji, located deep in the mountains on the coast of the Sea of Japan.

Jobs is known to have had no qualms about raising his voice if he didn't like something and was never the compromising sort. He didn't like things that were excessive, and he didn't like complications. It's interesting to imagine that Japanese culture may have been a part of the underlying spirit of the biggest company in the world. And today, the ownership rate of the iPhone is particularly high in Japan, which means that through

Steve Jobs, our minimalist culture has been imported right back to our country.

The definition of a minimalist

How do we define a minimalist? How far do you have to go in reducing your material possessions to call yourself a minimalist? It's tough to come up with an exact definition of a minimalist as there are bound to be elements that we'll end up missing, but my definition of a minimalist is a person who knows what is truly essential for him- or herself, who reduces the number of possessions that they have for the sake of things that are really important to them.

There are no set rules. It's not like you're disqualified if you own a TV or have more than a hundred possessions, or that you would then become a minimalist if you just got rid of those items. You're not even necessarily a minimalist just because everything you own can be stuffed into a single suitcase.

Different people have different approaches for their living environment. Satoshi Murakami lives the life of a nomad, carrying around his homemade Styrofoam house. Keigo Sakatsume has no home, and he lives on the road with a tote bag as his sole possession.

My feeling is that minimalists are people who know what's truly necessary for them versus what they may want for the sake of appearance, and they're not afraid to cut down on everything in the second category.

The things that are important to you will vary. The process of reducing your other items will also vary. So I don't think there's a single correct answer to the question of what makes a person a minimalist.

Minimalism is not a goal

Reducing the number of possessions that you have is not a goal unto itself. I think minimalism is a method for individuals to find the things that are genuinely important to them. It's a prologue for crafting your own unique story. In this book, I'd like to share the things that I've personally become more aware of by reducing the bulk of my material possessions.

I would also like to talk about minimalism for things besides material objects. In today's busy world, everything is so complicated that minimalism, which began with objects, is spreading to other areas as well.

It's an attempt to reduce the things that aren't essential so we can appreciate the things that really are precious to us.

It's a simple idea that we can apply to every facet of our lives.

Who is the ultimate minimalist?

There are various opinions on when minimalism first began, who may have coined the term, and who might have been the ultimate minimalist. I'm not sure the question matters much, but it's intriguing to think about.

I think Steve Jobs was one example of a perfect minimalist. Mother Teresa was another. I've heard that when she passed away, all she left behind was a well-worn sari, a cardigan, an old bag, and a pair of worn-out sandals. Mahatma Gandhi, a man of nonpossession, was also said to have left behind very sparse living quarters. Consider the ancient Greek philosopher Diogenes of Sinope. Diogenes is said to have owned only the sheet of cloth that he wore and a wooden bowl—which he shattered one day when he saw a peasant child drink from the hollow of his hands.

As you can see, minimalism has been around for quite a while. Diogenes may very well be the ultimate minimalist—it's hard to beat one sheet of cloth—but we don't need to go to such an extreme to experience the comfort that minimalism can bring us.

Danshari and the rise of modern minimalism

Around 2010, certain concepts began to create buzz in Japan:

1. *Danshari*, the art of de-cluttering, discarding, and parting with your possessions
2. The "simple life"
3. Working and thinking like a nomad

The Life-Changing Magic of Tidying Up by Marie Kondo was published in 2010 and became a smash hit, and many minimalists have since emerged in Japan. In my humble opinion, there were a few things happening in the background that led to this:

1. Information and material overload
2. The development of technology and services that make it possible for us to live without as many possessions as we had in the past
3. The Great East Japan Earthquake

I believe these key factors prompted people to start reconsidering the way they lived. Let's look at them one by one.

Too much information to handle

First, there's information and material overload. For better or worse, globalization has become a key part of our society. All we have to do is take a look at our smartphones to get the news from all corners of the globe. We can buy anything we want online, anywhere in the world. We can watch TV shows from any foreign country, not to mention listen to overseas radio shows.

It's almost as if all my friends have become essay writers or gourmet reporters, or maybe foreign correspondents, when I think of all the latest information they send me from wherever they are through Twitter, Facebook, and LINE. It isn't just friends; you can use social media to enjoy an endless stream of content being posted by people throughout the world.

According to 2014 data,* 306 hours of video content are uploaded to YouTube, 433,000 Tweets are posted on Twitter, and 50,000 apps are downloaded from the App Store every minute. The information at our fingertips is increasing at an astounding rate. I heard somewhere that the amount of information that a person living in Japan receives in a single day is equivalent to what someone who lived during the Edo period received in a year, if not over the course of their entire life.

Human beings are like fifty-thousand-year-old pieces of hardware

I've also heard that we humans are like pieces of hardware that haven't changed for fifty thousand years. Think about all the changes just since the Edo period four centuries ago, and then consider that we're coping with all that with a brain that's fifty thousand years old!

It isn't as if a company like Apple can come up with a clever innovation and say to us one day: "We've reconsidered the features of human beings and have created a new design. Our brains function thirty percent faster than the older version and our memory capacity has doubled. Our height has increased by three centimeters and our weight has decreased by two kilograms.

---

* "In an Internet Minute—2013 vs. 2014," Tech Spartan, accessed October 7, 2016, http://www.techspartan.co.uk/features/internet-minute-2013-vs-2014-infographic/.

Ladies and gentlemen, the moment you've all been waiting for—introducing 'iHuman2'!"

Without an upgrade like that, we're stuck filling up our old hardware with too much information and too many things. Our limited hard disk space is overloaded with unnecessary information. Our precious memory is consumed with how others see us, and it's used mostly for chasing things and managing them. We turn to all sorts of entertainment for temporary relief. And eventually, even that becomes too overwhelming and we start to reach for the easiest and most mindless distractions like smartphone games, gossip, and alcohol. I can tell you this because these are exactly what I used to reach out to.

I was like a slow computer that kept going around in circles

I used to be a slow computer where you'd see the loading icon spinning on the screen for what seemed like an eternity. I was up to my ears in data, and even if I wanted to try something new, there was so much that had to be done simultaneously that I would probably crash immediately. That's possibly why I was only able to handle menial tasks back then.

About sixty thousand different thoughts are said to go through a person's mind over the course of a day. Ninety-five percent of that is made up of the same things we'd been thinking about the day before, and 80 percent of those thoughts are believed to be negative.

In my days as a maximalist, I lived in fear of my future, constantly worrying about my career and how others saw me. Forget about that 80 percent I mentioned a moment earlier—practically all my thoughts were negative.

So, how do you make a slow computer like that work properly? Since our fifty-thousand-year-old hardware isn't going to change, we need to get rid of the extra load that isn't needed. Rather than trying to add more and more, running out of disk space and exhausting ourselves in the process, I think it's time we started thinking about subtracting and refining to enhance the truly important things that might be buried deep down underneath all that excess.

We can do anything on our smartphones

The second thing I'd like to point out is that, thanks to the advancement of technology and services, we can now get by without actually owning a lot of things.

The invention of the smartphone means we can carry around a cell phone, camera, TV, audio device, game console, watch, calendar, flashlight, map, or even notepad, all in one little rectangle. It's also a compass, train timetable, dictionary, thick mail-order catalog, checkbook, or airline ticket. The first iPhone was introduced in Japan in 2007. I think the invention of the smartphone paved the way for all the minimalists we see around us today. No matter how vigorously a minimalist may throw away their possessions, their smartphone is often one of the last items to go (if it goes at all), because it obviously serves so many different functions.

More technology helps us minimize

I mentioned earlier that I've always had an avid interest in photography. I never went anywhere without a compact film camera in my bag, and the negatives and prints I developed took up considerable space in my closet. When I proceeded with my *danshari*, my scanner was absolutely indispensable. I scanned all my negatives and prints and then threw them away. I was also able to scan and part with the letters I'd saved since kindergarten, greeting cards, and magazines that I just couldn't throw away. My ScanSnap scanner allowed me to say goodbye to an enormous amount of files and pictures, and still make it quick and easy to create data files and call them up on my computer.

There are probably a lot of people who listen to music only on their smartphones or iPods. I have a MacBook Air, which can be used to watch movies, listen to music, or read books. Though I no longer own a TV, I can visit the websites for TV networks and purchase archived programs that I'd like to watch. E-mail can be checked anywhere with my Gmail account, and I can work wherever I am by storing my files using cloud storage services like Dropbox. Wi-Fi infrastructure and Bluetooth connections have reduced the hassle of carrying around cables, and meetings can be done on Skype. We live in a wonderful world now where we can work without a physical office at all.

The spread of a sharing culture

Minimalist technology has expanded to include services as well. I live in Tokyo where traffic is always a nightmare and the public transportation system is very reliable, so there's really no need to own a car. Car sharing is good enough for me. It's economical: You don't have to pay car ownership taxes, there's no need to worry about paying maintenance fees, and it's easier on the environment. I have no doubt that we'll be seeing more of this trend, even outside of cities, in the future.

We're seeing the spread of a new sharing culture with our living spaces as well. There are services available today like Couchsurfing and Airbnb that allow us to rent out our houses and apartments to travelers from around the world. The Internet has made it possible for us to offer our resources to people who need them, and to receive resources from others in turn.

The physical danger of our possessions

Last, the Great East Japan Earthquake not only affected our sense of value, I think it prompted a big change in how we look at our possessions.

Mai Yururi is an artist whose comic format essay series, *Watashi no uchi niwa nanimo nai* (There's Nothing in My House), became a big hit. I was one of the many people who had been shocked to see pictures of Mai's sparse home. She's been given the nickname *Sute-hentai* (Weirdo Obsessed with Throwing Things Away). One scene in her book made a real impression on me: All the possessions that she and her family had lovingly kept in their home came crashing down when the earthquake struck and turned into deadly weapons. All of their cherished objects were washed away by the tsunami. Everything had been ruined.

The Great East Japan Earthquake was said to be so large that it should only happen once every thousand years. I recall hearing someone say that our history from the year 0 through 2000 is the equivalent of twenty old ladies living to the age of one hundred. If that earthquake really was a once-in-a-thousand-years event, it would mean that two of those twenty old ladies would have been affected. Is that a high ratio or is it low?

Considering the rise of information overload, the advance of technology, and the increasing occurrence of deadly natural disasters, I can't help wondering if the rise of minimalism in recent years may have been inevitable. Minimalism *had* to be born, not out of a mere spur-of-the-moment idea or yearning for a new lifestyle, but from an earnest desire and fervent need to rethink our lives.

2

Why did we accumulate so much in the first place?

I had everything I wanted . . .

I never realized before that I already had everything I needed to live a decent life. I kept wanting more and never felt satisfied. Often we think that our reality is so far removed from our ideal lifestyle that we must have suffered some misfortune along the way. But all that does is make us unhappy.

I'd look around my apartment and sigh. I don't have a nice leather couch or a spacious living room, and I don't have a big terrace where I can have barbecues. I don't own a high-rise apartment that offers a great view of the city. I didn't have any of the things that I thought I had always wanted.

It turns out, however, that the complete opposite was true: I actually already had everything I ever wanted. Allow me to explain.

Take our jobs, for example. We all work at a company that at some point we wanted to join. We went through some screening process and were accepted. Maybe it wasn't your number one choice or the industry that you really wanted to get into, but you needed a job. And because there's always been that niggling feeling deep down that maybe you compromised, you can't help complaining about your work or your boss. You can't help wondering what a career change might be like.

But it's worth remembering that at some point you really wished you could work there. Maybe the company culture isn't what you expected. Maybe your boss is a nightmare, or worse, the whole management is corrupt. Even so, you sent them your resume and showed up at the interview not because you had to, but because you wanted to. So in that sense, your wish to work at that company came true. You must have been happy, even if just for a little while, to receive that offer letter.

The same can be said for where we live. I lived in my old apartment for ten years. It was a great bargain that I'd found after searching and searching, and I can still remember the joy I felt when I first moved in. It was located in an area where I had longed to live, and I had been filled with a sense of anticipation that my new life was about to begin. But as the years went by, I started noticing how small and old the apartment was and my dissatisfaction gradually began to mount. Why was I feeling so unhappy when my previous wish to live there had been fulfilled?

The same goes for our belongings. Take our clothes, for example. I often felt like I didn't have anything decent to wear. I'd spend my off days shopping and come home exhausted but happy to have found something that I liked (even if maybe I'd used my credit card to splurge a bit). Then I'd put on a fashion show in front of my mirror. I would feel happy and proud the next day, sporting my new outfit. There had to have been days like that for all my clothes, so why is it that I now look in my closet and sigh, thinking that I don't have anything nice to wear?

When we look at things this way, we realize that many of our wishes have actually been granted. So why don't we feel satisfied? Why do we become unhappy?

We get used to things

We all know the answer to that question. We eventually get used to the new state where our wishes have been fulfilled. We start taking those things for granted, and there comes a time when we start getting tired of what we have.

Any woman would probably be happy when she puts on a brand new dress for the first time. But by the fifth time, she's probably gotten used to that dress and feels less thrilled when she wears it. After the tenth time, it's no longer a new dress. It's something she's gotten used to seeing hanging in her closet. Maybe she'll get tired of it after wearing it fifty times. The glory of acquisition starts to dim with use, eventually changing to boredom as the item no longer elicits even a bit of excitement. This is the pattern of everything in our lives. No matter how much we wish for something, over time it becomes a normal part of our lives, and then a tired old item that bores us, even though we did actually get our wish. And we end up being unhappy.

In other words, we can continue being happy if we can maintain that sense of joy that we experienced when we initially fulfilled our wish. If we could just be satisfied with what we have, then we wouldn't have to keep buying more and better things. So why can't we help becoming bored of things that become familiar?

Why do we keep wanting new things?

Our boredom with familiar things springs from certain aspects of our neural networks. Our neural networks are what allow us to detect variances in different forms of stimulation.

For example, imagine the sea in autumn. The summer beach season has long since ended but you suddenly have the impulse to do something youthful and you run into the water in your bare feet. The cold water makes you cry out. This is because your neural network has recognized the difference in the temperatures of the sand and the water. But if you stay in the water, you'll gradually get used to this new temperature and it'll stop bothering you. And you might then say to yourself, "Maybe it isn't as cold as I thought."

It's the same thing for a person who's asleep on a couch in front of a TV. They wake up the moment you turn it off and they complain, "Hey, I was watching that!" Though it's actually more relaxing with the TV turned off, they had gotten used to the bright screen and the constant noise as they fell asleep and instantly recognized when that stimulus was removed.

Variances or changes are necessary for people to recognize stimuli. This is why we often find ourselves unhappy after we've owned something for a while. Although we initially had a desire for it, our brain recognizes a lack of this variance once we get used to having it. The novelty of the new stimulus wears off, and the item becomes a part of our lives that we now take for granted. Without that variance, we eventually get sick and tired of it.

The enormous power of this effect can poison everything. It can make the clothes we'd seen at a boutique and pined for eventually look terribly unattractive and make us complain that we don't have a thing to wear. It can make us forget the joy we used to feel in doing our jobs. A person can get a face lift, become bored of the enhancements, and continue to have more and more work done. A child's face might light up when you give them a toy ring or a toy car. But they'll eventually get bored and maybe now that ring needs to be a $500 ring, then a $3,000 ring, then a one-of-a-kind ring created by a master. Maybe that toy car becomes a domestic car as a grown-up, then a luxury car, then a garage filled with a whole line of luxury cars. Don't you ever wonder about those rich people who have so much and yet continue to buy new things? Just like us, they get tired of having the same items, no matter how classy those items seem to us.

Why you can't cheer up Keisuke Honda after his World Cup defeat

There's a complication about this familiarity conundrum that's worth mentioning: it's only the person in question who's going to be affected. The $500 ring and the domestic car may look perfectly fine to others, but their owners are still tired of them and unhappy. This is because stimulus variances can only be felt inside us.

As one example, let's take Keisuke Honda, a famous Japanese soccer player who suffered crushing defeats at the FIFA World Cup. Say he's sitting in his locker room totally depressed. I might approach him, put my hand on his shoulder, and say,

> Okay, you lost the match, but so what? Cheer up. You're still paid hundreds of millions and you drive around in your cool Ferrari. You could retire right now and travel the world, and I'm sure you'd never have a problem finding a great job as a coach. You have no concerns about your future, right? Compare yourself with me. So brighten up already.

There's no way that he'd be satisfied with comments like that, though, right? You can only make comparisons with your own stimulus levels; you can't notice variances from the stimuli of others. At his level, Honda can't be happy unless he wins his matches.

The joy of victory only lasts three hours?

People are known to get used to their stimuli terribly quickly. In an interview after Wimbledon in 1992, former world number one tennis player Andre Agassi said that he learned something that only few people are aware of: the joy of victory isn't nearly as strong as the despair you experience in defeat, and those happy feelings after winning are fleeting compared with how long you suffer from a crushing defeat.

Tal Ben-Shahar, a popular Harvard lecturer in positive psychology, became Israeli national squash champion at the age of sixteen. His five years of six-hour daily practices paid off. But once he got home after the victory ceremony, he realized that the joy had worn off and he was left with a feeling of emptiness. He told people that the happiness lasted for only three hours.

Only a handful of people get to experience the monumental joy of big achievements like these. And yet, even those few people quickly get used to such feelings of contentment.

Can Bill Gates eat six meals in a single day?

Sadly, whether you buy a ring that costs $100, $500, or $3,000, the level of happiness that you'll feel is basically the same. You aren't likely to be five times happier when you get a $500 ring as opposed to one that costs $100. Your smile isn't going to be five times larger, and you aren't going to be happier for five times as long. While there are no limits to the prices that come attached to objects, there are limits to our emotions, for sure.

If a $500 ring really could bring us five times the joy of a $100 ring, money and possessions would ensure lasting happiness. But no matter how rich you become, no matter how many things you own, the joy from all your things won't be much different from how you feel now. There are emotional limitations to the feelings of happiness that we're able to experience when we obtain something for the first time.

In the same way, we also have physical limitations. Even if you become rich like Bill Gates, the size of your stomach isn't going to change. You can't eat six fabulous meals in a day just because you've become Bill Gates. (Well, you can, but you certainly won't feel twice as happy as when you had three meals a day.) Getting rich doesn't mean that you'll receive a special bonus and your days will become twenty-five hours long instead of twenty-four.

The functions of a $20,000 Apple watch

The same thing can be said for the functions of objects. A $100,000 sports car will not have ten times the speed of a $10,000 compact car, and the law wouldn't allow it anyway. A $20,000 Apple watch won't have fifty times the battery life of a $400 Apple watch, and it won't have fifty times the processing speed, either.

If the functionality of products increased in line with their prices and if expensive cars could take us wherever we wanted at double or triple the speed, or if a down jacket that costs double what we now have offered double the warmth, why, money and objects could have made us all very happy! But unfortunately, that is not the case.

You can't predict your future feelings

Here's another question that I sometimes wonder about. We know that as we acquire things, we'll eventually end up growing tired of them. So shouldn't there come a point when we realize that there is no point to acquiring something new? Why do we never get tired of this cycle? Why do we continue building our stockpile?

I think the answer to that might be because we use the present as the basis for predicting our future emotions. While we may be the only form of life that has the ability to imagine the future, our predictions are far from accurate.

Have you ever gone to the supermarket when you're hungry and ended up buying more than you needed? Have you ever ordered too much at a restaurant when you sat at your table feeling very hungry? Your present state of hunger made you miscalculate how you'd be feeling once you started eating. We can't even anticipate our state of hunger a mere thirty minutes from now.

Many of us have experienced a terrible hangover at one time or another, and I think all of us have probably vowed never to drink so much again when our heads are pounding like mad. But once that headache becomes a distant memory, I'm probably not the only one who gets carried away again with those enticing but dangerous drinks.

It's hard for us to imagine the pleasures of sitting in front of a fire when it's a hot, humid day. It's also hard to imagine the refreshing comfort you get from an air conditioner when it's a freezing cold winter night. Or, to use Daniel Gilbert's example from his book *Stumbling on Happiness*, young people get a Deathlok tattoo because they think it's going to be cool forever. Although we've all enjoyed such experiences (perhaps the Deathlok example isn't as universal), we tend to consider our future based on our present.

The joy of wearing a jacket for the tenth time

What does this mean when it comes to our belongings?

Let's go back to our clothing example. We go shopping, finally find the jacket that we've been looking for, and we're so overjoyed that we don't even worry about the price tag. It's fantastic no matter how we look at it, especially when we compare it with the worn-out jacket that we're now wearing. We pay for it, take it home, and feel the same sense of contentment when we put it on and stand in front of the mirror.

The unfortunate thing is that although we can easily imagine how we're going to feel the first time we wear it, we are unable to imagine how we're going to feel when we wear it for the tenth time, or when we put it on a year after buying it.

It's hard for us to accurately forecast how our feelings will change from our initial joy when we buy it, to familiarity, and later to boredom. At the outset, when we don't actually own the jacket, it seems like the joy could simply go on forever.

Let's take a moment, now that we've covered several reasons for why we naturally collect things, to connect them all together. We have everything we thought we wanted in the past. Everything around us is an item that we had genuinely desired at one point or another. But regardless of the level of our desire at the time, we get used to these items and eventually lose interest. And then we develop a desire to have something else—a different stimulus, something more expensive for greater impact. We want more stimuli and continue to acquire more and more.

Even if your belongings seem sufficient to other people, your own perception is the only one that matters; you're the only one who can create those changes in stimuli. A domestic car that costs $10,000 can meet anyone's needs, but its owner will still become unhappy after he's bought it.

And even if you work hard to create that variance by acquiring the next item, the sense of happiness that you feel won't be much different from what you're now feeling. There are limits to the amount of happiness that you can feel, and a ridiculously expensive item is not going to make you ridiculously happy. A $500 ring won't bring you five times as much joy as would a $100 ring.

In the same way that your joy does not equal the price of an item you buy, neither do the functions of that item. A down jacket that costs double the price of the one you already have will not offer double the warmth. Your dissatisfaction continues, and you reach out for something else. You know you'll get used to the next thing and become tired of it as well, but you can't help predicting the future based on your present feelings.

You get stuck in this eternal loop and the number of possessions you have continues to increase. In the back of your mind you know that you'll never be satisfied, but you keep thinking that maybe this time the brief sense of happiness you feel will be the real thing. These are the mechanics of unhappiness, and they exist no matter how much you spend, no matter how much you own.

From prehistoric function to modern value

There's another, deeper reason for why we've accumulated so much. Long ago, people used things that were made of stone. Though they may look primitive to us today, those tools were ingenious innovations that offered fabulous functionality.

Stone tools saved us time and energy. Though it may have taken someone a whole day to create a single stone instrument, it became less time-consuming and easier for us to find and prepare food every day after that. And once a tool was created, no further efforts were required to maintain them. Thus they became necessities.

Earthenware was also created for purely functional reasons. Without modern luxuries like the supermarkets and convenience stores that we take for granted today, early humans never knew when, or whether, food would be available. There was nothing they could do in the event of a natural disaster; they weren't even sure what would happen in the next moment. So they decided to store their leftover food, and thus earthenware items became a necessity.

With the passing of time, more and more of the items that we own today are used for purposes other than their functionality. Often it costs us enormous amounts of money and effort to maintain these items. These items aren't like the stone tools our ancestors had used, which faithfully served the purposes of their owners. They have begun to turn on us, and they've ended up ruling us before we realized it.

Why do we own so many things when we don't need them? What is their purpose? I think the answer is quite clear: We're desperate to convey our own worth, our own value to others. We use objects to tell people just how valuable we are.

We all have an app installed that recognizes loneliness

Let's take a look at this from the beginning again. We evolved as social animals. Compared with larger animals, our physical strength isn't that great and we don't have sharp claws or fangs. There's probably never been a person who could hunt a gigantic mammoth single-handedly. So in order to survive, we had to work in packs.

This pack mentality is still with us today. It's like we're preinstalled with an app that recognizes loneliness, and causes us to feel lonely when we're separated from our pack. This app is like an alert device that tells us to go back and join the others when we're all alone. And unfortunately, we can't remove this app; it's installed by default and cannot be deleted.

The loneliness of cats and dogs

Have you ever thought about the differences between cats and dogs? Though a cat can stay at home alone and be perfectly comfortable, this is not the case for a dog. Leave the dog alone for an extended period and it'll probably start barking or walking in circles by the door. It's known that dogs that have been in solitude for a long period can suffer depression.

Unfortunately, we're more like dogs, not cats. We've been designed to act in packs and avoid solitude.

As social animals, we feel the need to have value to society. We're unable to live without feeling that there's some meaning to our existence through the recognition or acknowledgment of others.

One of the main reasons we become depressed or consider committing suicide is that we convince ourselves of the lack of value of our existence. There are said to be a million people in Japan who suffer from depression and more than twenty-five thousand who commit suicide each year. When you consider that approximately twenty thousand people were victims of the Great East Japan Earthquake, a major catastrophe that's believed to occur once in a thousand years, we need to ask why it is that a larger number of people resort to taking their own lives year after year.

To me, this is a clear sign of how strong the human desire to affirm our own worth is. I think it follows closely after physiological desires like our appetite and our desire to sleep—and it permeates all aspects of our behavior. People can't manage to go on in this world if they don't believe in their own worth. A small amount of self-appreciation and narcissism is indispensable for us to live.

Some may say, "It's up to us to determine our own value," and I agree to some extent, but if we're completely alone and never see anyone or connect with others, then there's no way for us to affirm our worth. I think that no matter how much of a lone wolf someone may appear to be, there's some level of desire within them to have another person—anyone—turn their attention to them. Like dogs, we simply can't bear absolute loneliness. Unless we can see ourselves reflected from another person's perspective, it isn't possible for us to really know our worth.

Our self-worth drives our behavior

You may think I'm exaggerating, but I believe self-worth lies at the base of nearly all our actions.

We're pleased when someone "likes" something we share on social media. We're happy when someone follows us. They've recognized our worth.

We're very happy when someone we love loves us back. It's fantastic when the person that we love—the person who we feel has the most value to us—recognizes us. And we get upset if they two-time us, if they share that love with someone else.

"You're a terrible person! Who is this other person who's

better than me?" we might scream at him or her if we're jilted. "I hope it was *worth* it!"

Or perhaps you're rich, and want to make sure people know it. You have a chauffeur and you have him open the car door for you as you get out and walk around feeling important, wearing sunglasses, gold jewelry, and intimidating others as you're followed around by your subordinates. "Make way! I'm important!"

This is also the case when we say to someone that we're useless. We're waiting for them to say, "No, you aren't. You're worthy." Other times, we criticize others, bringing them down to affirm our own worth in the process.

It's also partly why I wrote this book. Though it isn't my sole motivation, I want to prove to myself that there's some kind of value to my existence.

Being the social animals that we are, we can't live without thinking that we have value. We can't do anything without a reasonable dose of narcissism. So it isn't a bad thing to think that we're worthy. In fact, it's necessary.

The problem lies in *how* we convey our value to others.

Conveying our self-worth

People have different types of qualities. Some of them are immediately apparent from our appearance. Maybe you're slim or cute, or perhaps you're tall, muscular, beautiful, fashionable, or have a fantastic figure. External appearances are easy to grasp; anyone can understand the message at a glance. But no matter how we polish the surface, there's a limit to how much we can do. I'm never going to look like a gorgeous fashion model.

There are other forms of qualities inside us as well. We might be kind, generous, funny, hardworking, sincere, cheerful, conscientious, smart, thoughtful, or courageous.

But these types of qualities are hard to convey to other people. Maybe a person who appears to be kind wouldn't be so reliable when they're faced with an emergency. Maybe someone who seems bright and interesting is actually quite self-centered. Unless we spend some time with another person, it's often tough to see their true worth.

This is where our belongings come into the picture. We can use items to communicate our personality and our values.

Clothes are a good example. A rock-star outfit will show that we're not afraid to be different, while a more natural style will convey a personality that's kind and gentle. High fashion might highlight our avant-garde sensitivities, while casual dress may communicate that we're frank and friendly. And if we're not too fussy when it comes to fashion, we convey the message that we aren't concerned about appearances. A good taste in furniture, a precious antique collection, the posters we have hanging on our walls, the plants that we grow in our garden—all of these are items that convey a sense of our values.

I'm a fan of Apple products. I think their functionality is excellent. Once I get hold of a new iPhone on its launch day, I want to flaunt it to my friends. I might want to casually open up my MacBook Air at Starbucks. There's definitely a part of me that wants to show off my worth as someone who chooses Apple products and can appreciate their great designs and usability. I think this type of urge is natural and there's nothing wrong with it, in and of itself.

When what we own becomes who we are

The problem starts to occur when we buy things just to convey our qualities to others, and our collections start to grow too big.

The more we accumulate and the harder we work to build a collection that communicates our qualities, the more our possessions themselves will start to become the qualities that we embrace. In other words, what we own equals who we are.

Our objective shifts to increasing our belongings, since that's the equivalent of increasing our self-image. As a result, we end up spending an enormous amount of time and energy to maintain and manage all these items that we've accumulated. When we consider these things as equivalent to our own qualities and start believing that they are in fact us, our number one objective will become their maintenance and management.

I believed that my bookshelves were a showcase of who I was

Here's an example from my life. I used to have books piled onto bookcases that took up all the space in my narrow hallway. Yet I could barely remember reading any of them. None of them became my flesh and blood. During my college days, I had been hungry for books that looked challenging. But many of them I just flipped through once without actually reading anything. There were books on modern philosophy and masterpieces of the twentieth century—very lengthy literary works—that I never finished reading.

It's clear to me now why I kept these books lying around and never got rid of them even though I knew I was never going to read them. I was desperate to convey my worth through my books. They were there to communicate one message:

I've read a lot of books to date. As anyone who looks at my bookshelves can see, my interests are diverse, and I'm very inquisitive. I know all about these different topics, if only in name. Though I haven't read all the books yet, I'm definitely interested in these areas—of course I am, that's why the books are sitting there on my bookshelf. I may not understand everything that's discussed in these books, but I've read huge volumes of works including an array of publications on complex issues. I'm not very talkative and I may look like a plain, ordinary guy, but inside I'm filled with all this incredible knowledge. Perhaps I can be described as an intellectual with depth.

As embarrassing as it is to admit it, that just about sums up why I had piles of books stacked up in my apartment. I was trying to show my worth through the sheer volume of the books I owned.

The same can be said for my mountains of CDs and DVDs. Ditto for my antique pieces, the stylish photographs that decorated the walls, my tableware, and my camera collection. I hardly ever used any of this stuff.

I had so many possessions I couldn't properly care for any of them. Because of all these things that I had, it was hard to clean the apartment, and the constant mess at home sapped my confidence and the drive to do anything. And I escaped with alcohol to avoid admitting this to myself. What an idiot I'd been.

When our tools become our masters

Before we move to the next chapter, let's put the whole picture together. Our possessions are supposed to be our tools. They were used for such purposes during the Stone Age. As time went by, our world became plentiful, and objects began to be used for another purpose: to enable us to affirm our own worth.

We are social animals that act in packs; we can't thrive without proving our existence has value. We need others to recognize our qualities so we can believe that our life is worth living.

To show this value, we communicate our qualities through our belongings.

But when we become too reliant on that method, we end up being surrounded by too many possessions. The objects that are supposed to *represent* our qualities become our qualities themselves. Then we start collecting more things because we feel like we'll become more substantial that way.

All these things eventually turn on us; we become slaves to our belongings, forced to spend time and energy caring for them. We lose ourselves in our possessions. Our tools become our masters.

These objects themselves have no power. We're the ones who have raised their status to become our equals or even greater, but they're actually nothing more than objects. They don't symbolize us and they aren't our masters. They used to be plain old tools. So why not consider hanging on to just the things that we really need?

In the next chapter, I'd like to talk about specific methods for parting with our belongings. I'm pretty sure that most of us have accumulated so much that we're ready to lose ourselves amid our possessions. I think you might find it worthwhile to try to distance yourself from all those things, at least once in your life.

Get ready to say goodbye to all those things that have been holding you back.

3

55 tips to help you say goodbye to your things

1: Discard the preconception that you can't discard your things.

There's no such thing as a person whose nature won't allow him or her to discard their things. We only think we're unable to part with our possessions. "Learned helplessness" is a term used in psychology that can explain what's happening here. Though we have the ability to get rid of things, we've given up trying because we've experienced a number of failures.

But we're all able to part with our things; we just need to become aware of the reasons why we've been unable to do this so far. It isn't because of your nature, and therefore you're certainly not to blame. You're simply inexperienced—that's all there is to it. You aren't familiar with the habit of discarding your possessions and you've gotten used to keeping them. I used to live in a filthy apartment, but now I live in a minimalist space. It wasn't a personality change I went through; I simply learned the techniques and developed a habit of getting rid of excess.

2: Discarding something takes skill.

In the same way that you won't wake up one morning and discover that you've suddenly become fluent in French if you've never even studied it, you can't become a master at *danshari*, or de-cluttering and parting, overnight. I've thrown away a lot, but it's taken me more than five years to do this. (It *is* possible to do it more quickly.)

The act of discarding things in itself does not take time. Day one, you throw out the garbage. Day two is for selling your books and CDs. Day three, you sell your electric appliances. Day four is for selling large pieces of furniture, or taking them to the donation center. A week is actually all the time you need to reduce your possessions, no matter how much you may have. It's not the act itself but the decision to act that takes time. In the same way that your skills in a foreign language will improve with practice, so will the act of getting rid of things. The more you do it, the less time it will take to decide, and the easier it will be to say goodbye to your things. It's actually a skill.

3: When you discard something, you gain more than you lose.

Though it may seem like reducing your possessions means you're losing out on something, I think it's best to reset our minds on that point. There are more things to gain from eliminating excess than you might imagine: time, space, freedom, and energy, for example. I'll get into more detail in chapter 4 but let me just tell you now that the list of the things you gain is really limitless.

You can't help but fixate on something that you're about to throw away because it's right in front of you. And the potential gains from this action aren't visible, so it's hard to be aware of them. But trust me, there is actually more to gain than there is to lose. Rather than thinking about the loss of everything you discard, direct your attention to the things that you'll be gaining.

4: Ask yourself why you can't part with your things.

There probably aren't many people who will suddenly decide to reduce the number of possessions that they have and become a minimalist overnight. As I said earlier, the act of discarding things is a skill. It'll be hard at first to place your possessions in a trash bag or put them up for sale. There are still a lot of items that I can't get around to throwing away myself. But it isn't something to be embarrassed about. And there's no need to get rid of everything at once. I think it's important to think about why there are some things that we can't part with.

Take a minute to really focus on each item you can't part with and ask yourself why. Is it because it was expensive? Is it because you feel guilty about throwing it away? Are you ashamed that you were never able to make good use of it? Do you feel bad for the person who gave it to you? Does it feel like you're throwing away a fond memory that is attached to it? Is your vanity preventing you from parting with something? Or is it just easier to leave it where it is?

Don't worry if you can't discard your possessions all at once. The important thing is to ask yourself why you may be reluctant to part with some of your belongings. You might be surprised by the answers.

5: Minimizing is difficult, but it's not impossible.

The Dutch philosopher Baruch de Spinoza observed that when people say something is impossible, they've already decided that they don't want to do it. Though we may have a sincere wish to part with all our excess things, our sense of comfort from owning them may be stronger.

We shouldn't rationalize this comfort by saying that because some item is full of memories, or it was given to us by a dear friend, that we simply can't let it go. Yes, such beautiful reasons may certainly exist, but often the key reason is that it would just be a lot of trouble to discard.

We tend to prefer the path of least resistance. Discarding something requires effort, and leaving it as is would definitely be the easy choice. But if we keep putting off the work of minimizing, we'll eventually end up surrounded by too much.

If you really want to live as a minimalist, you need to make that desire your top priority.

6: There are limits to the capacity of your brain, your energy, and your time.

I used to have multiple bank accounts and a lot of bank cards fattening up my wallet. While these were thin cards that didn't take up much physical space, they took up a lot of the memory I had available in my brain. How much did I have left in each account? When should I withdraw the funds in each? What if I lost a card and someone went ahead and used it? Just going to the police and reporting the loss would take up a lot of my time.

With our fifty-thousand-year-old brain hardware, we don't have the room to waste time or energy on those little cards, or really on any extra possessions. It's wiser to clean up our system and delete all the unnecessary data so we're free to function efficiently and happily.

7: Discard something right now.

Maybe you're thinking that you'll de-clutter right after you finish the project you're working on right now. Or you might say to yourself that you'll get to it someday after things settle down. But we all know that as long as we're ruled by our dear old possessions, that day will never come.

We think we can't become a minimalist until our lives have settled down. But it's actually the other way around; we won't be able to settle down until we're living a minimalist life. All that time we so desperately need is within our grasp, but we have to create it ourselves by saying goodbye to all those extra things. That's why it's a good idea to start now. Make it a top priority.

Discarding things may take some skill, but you don't have to perfect that skill before you start taking action. Don't wait until you've finished reading this book. The best way to go about it is to hone your skills as you part with your possessions. Why not close this book this very moment and discard something?

If you wait until you have the time, you'll never have the time. This is the first step, right now, toward a minimalist life.

8: There isn't a single item you'll regret throwing away.

Since the days of my old messy apartment, I think I've reduced my possessions to around 5 percent of what I used to own. That's 950 out of 1,000 items. And you know what? There really isn't a single item that I miss. Even if there had been such an item at the time, I can't even remember what it was. That's how insignificant all those things were to me. There really isn't a single item that I think about and pine over.

It seems to me that this fear of regret is what prevents us from saying goodbye. It's certainly understandable; we all have these types of fears. But if you're wondering whether you might need that ten-year-old jacket that's been sitting in the back of your closet forever, or those sea shells you picked up on the beach when you were a toddler, go ahead and tell yourself that there's probably not a single item that you'll regret throwing away.

9: Start with things that are clearly junk.

The best way to get used to discarding things is to make it a habit. Let's say you want to make it a habit to go jogging early in the morning. An effective way to do this is to aim to go to the door on the first day. The objective for the second day is to do that *and* put on your running shoes. You gradually keep adding to your small accomplishments to achieve a bigger objective. Ichiro Suzuki, one of the best baseball players in Japan and America, said the accumulation of small achievements is the only way to do something incredible. The same applies to throwing things away. Maybe you start by throwing away some old torn-up flip-flops. The next day, you get rid of some ancient boots with holes in the bottom. You feel emboldened and throw away your moldy old raincoat the next day. Bit by bit, you build on your achievements.

But before we get into any of that, a good basic first step is to start with what anyone would consider garbage. Throw away empty cans or food containers that aren't being used. Check your refrigerator and get rid of the expired food items. Discard clothes with holes in them. Throw away broken appliances. Start by clearing out the things that have clearly become junk.

10: Minimize anything you have in multiples.

It's easy to minimize things you have in multiple numbers. Go on, take a look. Do you have two or three pairs of scissors? Do you have a bunch of unused ballpoint pens? Two calligraphy paintbrushes? We often lose track of how many of the same items we have because we don't have a designated spot to keep them. That's often how we start cluttering up our space. And the more you have, the harder it is to know what you have.

If you have three pairs of scissors, you can start by throwing away one of them. It's easy to choose which one that will be: the pair you aren't particularly fond of or the pair that you don't use. You can still cut with fewer scissors. You can still write with fewer pens.

Try to reduce the multiples of anything you have to one.

11: Get rid of it if you haven't used it in a year.

One essential method for reducing your possessions is to discard things you haven't used in a year. You should also get rid of things you have no firm plans to use in the future. You don't need to throw away the blanket, or the down jacket, you're going to be using come winter. The same goes for the bathing suit you always wear in the summer.

But if you haven't used something during the past four seasons, you probably don't need it. The one exception would be the emergency equipment and supplies that you keep in case of a disaster.

Dust isn't very pleasant but it is a useful sign that tells us maybe it's time to consider throwing an item away. The heavier the layer of dust, the less we've used something. An item that you haven't used this past year probably won't suddenly become necessary next year or the year after that. And if there is something you happen to use once every three years, why not rent it when you need it? Let's free up all that time and energy we spend maintaining things that we never use.

12: Discard it if you have it for the sake of appearance.

As I wrote in chapter 2, we often try to use objects to show our worth. So you might ask yourself if you have some of your items because you're really fond of them, or if it's possibly because you're using them to reflect qualities of yourself that you want to highlight.

We're of course all concerned with how others see us. It feels good to present yourself as someone who enjoys a wonderful lifestyle surrounded by fancy kitchen items, beautiful furniture, a stylish car, and an expensive watch. Or maybe you have an image as a creative type who surrounds themself with art and musical instruments. Everyone goes the extra mile to project their intended image.

The possessions that we truly enjoy, however, are the things we use often that don't require a lot of effort to maintain. And while the trappings of a successful lifestyle are tempting, you might want to consider letting go of the things you keep just to show off to others.

13: Differentiate between things you want and things you need.

Here's an exaggerated example. You're climbing a mountain but you aren't well equipped. You're wearing thin clothing, you don't know anything about the environment, and you get lost. The temperature drops, it starts pouring rain, and you're trembling from the cold. Desperate, you finally find a small lodge where you step inside and warm your freezing body with a blanket. That blanket is an item that you truly need.

In our everyday lives, though, vast inventories of goods are available for sale just a short walk or drive away. On offer are the latest electrical appliances, stylish goods and accessories, gorgeous high-fashion apparel, and everything else we would ever want. A single warm blanket is enough when you're stranded on a mountain, and yet back at home you would probably want a second blanket in a nice color and then a third, higher-quality blanket with a more luxurious texture.

You can avoid buying more things simply by first asking yourself if it's something that you actually need. The Buddhist monk Ryunosuke Koike says he puts his hand against his chest when he's not sure about an item, and it will feel uncomfortable if the item is merely something that he wants. This discomfort is a symptom of dissatisfaction, of the mistaken belief that there's something missing from his life even though he already has everything he needs.

14: Take photos of the items that are tough to part with.

Call me sentimental, but I like to take pictures of the things I'm about to part with, to soften the blow. This is something that I still do from time to time—just the other day I took a picture of an old pair of nail clippers before I got rid of them. You're probably wondering what I do with these images. I don't think I've ever even looked at them myself. I take them to preserve the memories that are associated with these belongings.

I think throwing away your material possessions and throwing away your memories are two completely different actions. As long as you still have the images, you'll be able to recall your experiences. A work of art that your child made in grade school, a souvenir from a trip, or a gift that someone gave you—take pictures of them and it'll be easier to throw these things away when you feel like you can't. I can say from experience that it's very unlikely that you'll actually go back and look at the images. I've taken thousands of pictures and I think I'm just about ready to delete them. When I do, I know it'll mean that I've started to become more focused on the present. Until the day comes when I can discard unnecessary things without a second thought, I think I'll continue to snap away.

15: It's easier to revisit your memories once you go digital.

As a fan of film photography, there's no telling how much I spent on film and development costs. I always had my favorite compact camera tucked away in my bag and I loved taking pictures, but what I wasn't very good at was organizing the material afterward. The photo prints and the negatives were stuffed haphazardly in bags after I had them developed, and it was impossible to tell when they'd been taken. I put them away in my closet and it was a hassle to even pull them out.

Once I decided to go minimalist, I scanned all my prints on ScanSnap, as well as the letters I'd received from people over the years, and made everything digital. It's now easy to see them on my computer if the mood strikes, and with the dates and places included in the names of the folders, the materials make sense chronologically. And by backing everything up in cloud storage, I can access my precious albums wherever I may be in the world.

16: Our things are like roommates, except we pay their rent.

In Japan, it's said that you need half a tatami mat for someone to be seated and a full one (about sixteen square feet) for them to sleep. That's actually all the space we need to get by. If we added a roommate, it would just mean we need enough space for another tatami mat. In that sense, the rent wouldn't increase that much if a friend were to come live with you.

But whether or not someone is actually living with us, we all have a roommate. We call them "Our Things." And the space they need is far beyond that half or full tatami mat I just described.

We all would like to live in a nice, spacious home. But when you really think about it, we just want to allow Our Things to live in a comfortable environment. And what do we get in return? Our Things aren't going to pitch in with the rent, and they aren't going to help us take care of the household chores. Instead, they create extra work for us. Do we really want to continue to pay the rent for them? It's wiser to kick them out.

17: Organizing is not minimizing.

We Japanese have a custom of tackling major housecleaning at the end of the year. We throw some things out, we clean up anything we have lying around, and we put it all out of sight. We attempt to make good use of unused space and stow our belongings so they won't get in the way as we go about our daily lives. But as time passes, we become busy with other things, and naturally, we're back with our clutter a year later. Unless we're extremely fastidious, we'll end up going through this cycle time and again. This is because organizing is not minimizing.

Instead of relying on organization techniques, you should first focus on decreasing the amount of things you have to put away. Once you do that, your space will naturally become less cluttered; the cycle will be broken. I have so few items in my apartment, it simply doesn't get cluttered. The concept of clutter itself has left me!

18: Tackle the nest (storage) before the pest (clutter).

Here's a huge tip for throwing things away. Normally, we clean up by gradually reducing the clutter in our storage space, after which we are finally able to throw away our storage containers themselves.

But let's take a moment to think about how we get rid of household pests. Do we go about killing insects one by one and then finally get started on the nest after such a tedious process? Of course not; those pests will be multiplying faster than we eliminate them.

The same can be said for the nests that we call storage. Even if we clear it out thoroughly, we'll eventually start filling it up again. So the most effective method for cleaning up is to do away with the nest itself.

Get rid of our storage containers? I can sense your skepticism from here. Our possessions are going to be scattered all over the place if we don't have a proper place to store them. They'll wind up sitting around in piles. Fortunately, most of us can't bear such a sight and we'll feel compelled to do something about it, like start throwing things away. When our possessions no longer have a comfortable home, they'll be just like those pesky insects without a nest—they'll eventually start to disappear.

19: Leave your "unused" space empty.

When we talk about home organization, the concept of "unused" space becomes important. We see an area where we haven't put anything, and we think of it as unused space. Naturally, we put our various skills to use and try to fill the void.

For example, we set up our washing machines in a designated spot at home and then notice the unused space overhead. Particularly with the limited size of apartments in Tokyo, we try to make efficient use of what we have. So what we often do is set up a rack over our washing machines where we can store towels, laundry detergent, fabric softener, bleach, and so on.

But of course that isn't the end of it. We often put up a pole from one wall to another, place hangers and hooks onto it, and rejoice in the ingenious storage space that we've created. But this is actually a step away from downsizing, from living in comfort. Once we have extra storage space, we inevitably start to store extra things. The items on that pole will eventually start to overflow.

A storage area packed with our possessions is like a crowded commuter train. It isn't a soothing sight. And it takes more time and effort than we think to maintain its initial state. It's actually open space, left empty, that gives us peace of mind. While your brain may at first think of them as "unused" spaces, these open areas are incredibly useful. They bring us a sense of freedom and keep our minds open to the more important things in life.

20: Let go of the idea of "someday."

When we buy an electrical appliance, it usually comes with a lot of attachments. Think of all those parts for your vacuum cleaner that you've never used. What's that little screw for, anyway? You keep all those parts and wires because you think you might need them "someday." I don't know about you, but I've never actually used a warranty. They now go straight into the trash can.

We're always thinking about "someday." We keep empty cookie tins or beautiful paper bags, thinking they might come in handy someday. We hold on to foreign language textbooks because we're going to start studying someday. We'll get to all those hobby items and tools once things quiet down. Someday. That's what we tell ourselves. But we know by now that that time is probably never going to come. May I make a gentle suggestion? Let go of "someday." Things we don't need now will probably never be needed.

21: Say goodbye to who you used to be.

When discarding anything, it's important to consider whether it is something that you need *right now*. In the same way that trying to prepare for someday in the future is futile, so is clinging to what used to be in the past.

The textbooks you used in school, the books that opened up your eyes to the world when you were a child, that favorite outfit that once made you shine—memories are wonderful, but you won't have room to develop if your attachment to the past is too strong. It's better to cut some of those ties so you can focus on what's important today.

Holding on to things from the past is the same as clinging to an image of yourself in the past. If you're the least bit interested in changing anything about yourself, I suggest you be brave and start letting things go. Leave only the items that you need moving forward from this very moment.

22: Discard the things you have already forgotten about.

I think the ideal minimalist is someone who can give a rundown of every item that they own. We should be able to recall our possessions if they're all necessary things that we use regularly, right? In other words, if we've forgotten that they even exist, then it's pretty obvious that we don't really need them.

When you're combing your apartment for things to discard, there will be times when you'll come across something and say to yourself, "What, I had *this?*" There are bound to be clothes tucked away in the bottom of your dresser or far back in your closet.

Or you might think, *Yeah, yeah, I remember buying these.* Naturally, you'll start wondering if those old items might work with your current wardrobe, but wait a minute. You've managed without them all this time. They wouldn't have been buried wherever you found them if they were things that you needed.

You won't need those knickknacks that fell into the narrow space between your TV stand and the wall. You would have desperately looked for them if they were important.

Do you have boxes you've left unopened since you moved into your current home? You probably won't be needing those, either. Boxes filled with things you've forgotten about can almost certainly be discarded without a second glance. Go ahead, open them up and take a look if you aren't sure. But don't forget what we just discussed.

23: Don't get creative when you're trying to discard things.

We can get amazingly creative when we don't want to part with something. For example, you might stop and say to yourself, "This empty cookie tin might appear to be useless, but wait . . . what if I were to reuse it as a container for storing my medications?"

"I really should say goodbye to this worn-out tote bag. . . . But hey, I could use it as a place to keep my paper bags!"

"This perfume bottle may be pretty, but it's about time I got rid of it. Oh, hold on, I've just come up with a splendid idea! I'll go to the hardware store—one of these days—and pick up the wires I need to hook it up as a beautiful lamp!"

Chances are, the beautiful lamp that you've just envisioned will never come to be. Most of these thoughts are desperate ideas that pop into our minds because we really don't want to part with our old possessions. We are never more creative than when we're trying to throw things out. No matter how fantastic these ideas might be, it's probably wiser to do your best to ignore them.

24: Let go of the idea of getting your money's worth.

One reason why we tend to think it's a waste to discard something is that the item might have been expensive when we first bought it. Somewhere in the back of our minds, we're thinking that we haven't gotten our money's worth yet. But the reality of the matter is that we most likely never will.

You may have an outfit in a color and design that you love, but the size isn't quite right. It's still like new, and you haven't gotten enough use out of it to justify what you paid for it. Of course it's hard to throw away something like that.

But what's really happening is that it's taking up space in your home and your mind. Every time you look at it, you can't help but think that it was a mistake to buy that gorgeous outfit in the first place. If you were to convert that psychological drain to a dollar amount, maybe it's small, less than a dollar a day. But it's certainly continuing to cost you.

Whether or not you have any interest in the stock market, you would probably agree that it's wiser to get rid of stocks if they continue to fall with no prospects of a rebound. The same can be said for the bulk of our possessions. We should let go of the concept of getting our money's worth, and cut our losses sooner rather than later. It's easier on your wallet in the long run, not to mention easier for maintaining peace of mind.

25: There's no need to stock up.

Most of us stock up on toilet paper, tissues, and paper towels. Those extra supplies will certainly come in handy if we ever run out; we won't need to go running to the store. Plus, sometimes we can save money if we buy in bulk. These are everyday necessities, and we'll be sure to use them, right?

But think about all the space that they're taking up in storage. And the more space you give them, the more they'll take up until it eventually gets to a point where you won't even know just how much you have stocked up.

Let's say you've made a stop at the drugstore on your way home from work and see Q-tips on sale.

"Do I have Q-tips at home? Oh, they're on sale today, so I'll just pick up a couple of packs," you tell yourself. And then you come home and are shocked to find you already had enough stocked up to open a pharmacy.

Here's an idea: Start by keeping just one extra package on hand. And then don't replenish it. You can go out and buy another package (just one) the next time you run out. It isn't very considerate to have a bunch of extra supplies just for yourself, especially in times of emergency. Let's get in the habit of not stocking up now.

26: Feeling the spark of joy will help you focus.

In her best-selling book on the magic of tidying up, Marie Kondo came up with the killer phrase about sparking joy. The simple method of touching objects and leaving only the things that spark joy can be very useful.

Things that you aren't in love with but cost you a lot of money, things that you have not been able to use well that have become more of a burden, things that you've worn down from overuse—these tend not to spark joy. This test can be quite reliable.

Paying attention to what sparks joy is a way to focus, not on the past or the future but on the present. It's simple enough, and requires minimal amounts of time. As the bar can be surprisingly high for something to spark your joy, possessions that we haven't been able to throw away for no particular reason will also make their way into the trash bag.

To throw things away, it's necessary to ask, "Does this object spark joy or not?" This is an effective way to become more aware of our senses.

As we minimize, and our focus strengthens, we may even be able to go beyond this question about sparking joy. We'll return to this idea in the next section.

27: Auction services are a quick way to part with your possessions.

I've used a number of auction services to let go of a lot of my possessions, including the clothes I've barely ever worn, my unused electrical appliances, and my cherished camera collection. I learned this important lesson from a piece of photography equipment—a combination film developer and photo printer—I used to own. It was something that I'd gotten at an auction for about 150,000 yen (about $1,500)—with a loan from a friend—but I never got around to using it. I hung on to it thinking that in spite of the trouble it would take to put it up for auction myself, I was bound to get at least a 100,000 yen (about $1,000) for it. But in the end, I developed an urge to get rid of it right away and ended up throwing it in the trash. Forget about the money I'd expected to collect for it—after all the time I'd held on to that printer, I ended up having to pay to get rid of it.

Since then, I've used a local auction service called QuickDo (there are others springing up around the world) where you simply fill out a form and they put your item up for auction. They charge handling fees but you don't have to worry about the hassles of selling or shipping it yourself. It's a very convenient service that allows you to quickly get rid of your stuff while you can sit back and enjoy watching the bidding.

28: Use auctions to take one last look at your things.

I was able to get rid of a considerable amount of my belongings through a local auction service. There are of course online auction sites as well, like Yahoo! Auctions, but they require a bit of effort—you have to take pictures of each of your items and fill out all the product information, not to mention ship the goods to your customer.

Kouta Itou, one of the people I introduced earlier, thinks this extra effort is actually what makes auctions the best way to part with your belongings. Kouta used to be surrounded by his musical instruments and gear, and got rid of them through auctions.

He recommends auctions because the effort of preparing photos and compiling descriptions of your possessions gives you the chance to revisit the feelings you had when you first obtained those things.

And then you can also think about the reasons why each item is no longer needed. The auction preparation leads you to reflect on what those possessions had once meant to you. Kouta says it's during these procedures that he promises to never again buy something he doesn't need. Saying goodbye to his things at auction lets him move forward.

29: Use a pickup service to get rid of your possessions.

Packing and shipping your stuff after auctions can be a hassle. There's an easier way: Consider a pickup service that comes to your door to collect your things. Though they don't pay as much as what you might get through an auction sale, these kinds of services are very convenient. Their people come to your home to buy your goods, and you don't even have to go to the trouble of packing them. I often use Takakuureru.com, where you can sell a huge variety of things. Depending on where you're located, you'll have other options, of course.

These were the people who came to my rescue when I wanted to get rid of larger possessions like my TV set. I don't know how the situation is abroad, but in Japan, you have to pay money if you want to scrap these types of items. They also bought my PS3 and my home theater setup. A used bookstore in Jimbocho, Tokyo, came and picked up my collection of more than a thousand books. While I could have had them offer individual quotes for each book, I accepted the proposed bulk price of 20,000 yen (about $200) for the whole deal. It's possible to minimize more carefully, but I think minimizing the *effort* it takes to minimize is often the key to success.

30: Don't get hung up on the prices that you initially paid.

When I bought my forty-two-inch plasma TV, I think it must have cost me about 80,000 yen (about $800). I sold it for 18,000 yen (about $180). As for my home theater setup, I paid 40,000 yen (about $400) for it and later sold it for 5,000 yen (about $50). I have to admit that I'd been expecting to sell these items at higher prices. They were in good condition, and I had only used them for about three years. But then I realized I'd been fixated on how much I paid when I first bought these products. It's hard to part with your possessions if you confuse their current values with their original prices.

A new car becomes a used car the day after you've bought it. In the same way, your possessions continue to lose value with the passage of time. Though we tend to put high price tags on our belongings, we should try to think objectively about their true value when they're turned over to other people. Let's forget the generous estimates when it comes to our possessions. That will make it easier to part with them.

31: Think of stores as your personal warehouses.

Author Daisuke Yosumi writes that we should consider stores as our personal warehouses. All those stores out there pay good sums of money to secure space so they can stock all sorts of goods for us, and they manage their items with care. Convenience stores welcome us around the clock. Yosumi suggests we should not think of these places as shops where we buy goods, but instead as our warehouses where we go to get something when we need it.

There's no need to build a storage shed at home, or stuff a storage room with a lot of things and end up feeling suffocated. And it's a waste of money to rent storage space. Japan offers a huge variety of shops, and I'm sure it's the same in other places as well. They're always welcoming, and they offer an excellent assortment of goods. Many of these "warehouses" are near our homes, with people waiting to greet us with smiles on their faces. Think of all the online retailers, too—they are also massive warehouses. With so many convenient warehouses all around us, why bother setting one up at home?

32: The city is our personal floor plan.

I can understand people's desires to have a big, comfortable couch in the middle of a big, comfortable living room. I wouldn't mind having something like that myself. But I don't think it has to be set up in our homes. My "living room" is a diner in my neighborhood that has couches that are always comfortable and inviting, not to mention clean and tidy, where I can sit and relax for as long as I like. There's another coffee shop I frequent where they never complain no matter how many hours I sit there and chat with friends over cups of freshly brewed coffee.

Believe me, I'm no hermit. I'd love to invite friends over for a hot pot, or prepare cool hors d'oeuvres for a fabulous party. But for the few times that I would host such an event, am I willing to increase the number of items that I own and pretend not to notice all the space they take up in my home? Of course not.

So this is what I say to my friends: "A hot pot party? Yeah, that sounds great. We can't do it at my place, though, since I don't have the equipment. But listen, I know of a place that serves terrific hot pots, so why don't we go there? We can have drinks at my place afterward if we want to keep the party going."

When your entire neighborhood is your floor plan, the possibilities will be endless.

33: Discard any possessions that you can't discuss with passion.

In one of his books,* Daisuke Yosumi wrote about this concept. The more you like your possessions, the more knowledgeable you'll become on the brands and their backgrounds. There is a sense of wonder to things that we truly value.

Why do we own a certain product when there are so many wonderful things to choose from? There had to be a good reason why it had to be that particular item.

An item chosen with passion represents perfection to us. Things we just happen to pick up, however, are easy candidates for disposal or replacement. We're bound to be less satisfied with all those other things we've unconsciously accumulated. I think our lives are better when our belongings stir our passions. As long as we stick to owning things that we really love, we aren't likely to want more.

---

* *Jiyuude aritsuzukeru tameni nijuudaide suterubeki gojuuno koto* (50 Things You Should Get Rid of in Your 20s to Stay Free)

34: If you lost it, would you buy it again?

A key way to gauge your passion for something you own is to ask yourself, "If I were to somehow lose this, would I want to buy it again at full price?"

If the answer is yes, that item is something that you truly love. It's a necessity for you.

On the other hand, if you aren't the least bit interested in buying that same item again, there's clearly something about the product that you dislike. Maybe you're keeping it because it's "good enough." But that's not good enough; say goodbye to those ho-hum things.

It's the things you'd be willing to buy again that give you true satisfaction.

35: If you can't remember how many presents you've given, don't worry about the gifts you've gotten.

Presents are very tough to discard. We feel guilty about throwing something away that someone gave us as a gift; it seems heartless. But take a moment to think about something *you* gave someone as a present. These things don't usually stay in our minds as clearly as the things we've been given.

I've never asked someone if they're using something that I gave them. And if one of my gifts turned out to be something useless for the recipient, I'd hope they would feel comfortable getting rid of it. The last thing I want is for my gift to take up space in their home.

If you have a gift at home that you feel guilty about not using, it's better to just come clean and part with it. If someone actually gets upset when they find out that you've thrown away something that they gave you in the past, it means they're not as concerned about your relationship in the present. In that case, you may want to distance yourself from that person anyway. I know I wouldn't want to become someone who can only convey feelings of love or friendship through material objects.

36: Try to imagine what the person who passed away would have wanted.

If gifts are tough, discarding the possessions of a loved one who's passed away seems impossible. We're so concerned about cherishing our memories with that person that we tend to hang on to things for which we have absolutely no use. Don't get me wrong; I think that's an incredibly beautiful, and truly human, sentiment. But imagine that you were the one who had passed on. Would you want the people you've left behind to be confused or troubled about something you left them? Wouldn't you want them to live freely and happily without worrying about material objects?

The Japanese painter Ryuzaburo Umehara left a will saying that there was no need for a funeral and that condolence offerings were not to be accepted. He wrote that the living should not be troubled for the sake of the deceased.

I think it's more meaningful to try to recall the words of a deceased friend or relative, or treasure the things they did for you while they were alive, than spend time managing their possessions.

37: Discarding memorabilia is not the same as discarding memories.

Tatsuya Nakazaki, a graphic novelist known for his work "Jimi-hen," is a person who is thorough when it comes to minimalism. This is what he wrote in his book *Motanai otoko* (The Man Who Doesn't Possess): "I don't think there's any relationship between our past and photographs, records, and diaries. Even if we were to throw away photos and records that are filled with memorable moments, the past continues to exist in our memories. I don't think it's such a big deal to throw away objects; it isn't as if we're throwing away our past. If we forget a certain memory, then it's probably something that's all right for us to forget, something unnecessary. All the important memories that we have inside us will naturally remain."

It's the memories that we can recall without the aid of objects that are truly important. By getting rid of our extra possessions, we'll start to remember the important things from our past without being distracted by all that excessive memorabilia.

38: Our biggest items trigger chain reactions.

Let's say we switched from having one smartphone to two. We should realize that we haven't just added a single smartphone to our lives. We might get a case for the new smartphone, put a protective sheet of film over it, buy a power charger, covers for the earphone jack, and of course a strap. Before you know it, we've accumulated five new items. Things tend to bring in more things.

And if we buy a computer, there's no limit to the extras that we'll probably end up buying: a desk, printer, scanner, USB memory sticks, an external hard drive, word processing software, cleaning tools, and so on. Conversely, we'll be able to get rid of a lot of items at once if we dispose of the initial source. When I sold my TV, I was also able to dispose of my PS3, the hard drive for recording, and the home theater set that connected it all. All the wires and adapters, including their power plugs, also went. If we work up the courage to get rid of our biggest possessions, there's a big payoff.

39: Our homes aren't museums; they don't need collections.

There are people who have outstanding collections worth pre-serving. A couple of examples are Shigeru Kashima, a researcher of literature and collector of expensive old books from France; and Shin Sofue, a designer who collects Soseki Natsume's liter-ary masterpiece *Botchan* in various printed editions. The collec-tions that these people have are genuinely priceless and worthy of a museum. Takuro Morinaga, an economist who is known for his penchant for toy cars, appears to have actually created a museum for his collection.

But for most of us, our collections aren't priceless, and they take up a lot of home space. The things that are truly valuable are bound to be professionally collected and properly stored by someone somewhere. When it comes to collections, be brave. Let them go. Our homes aren't museums. We can always visit a real museum to see rare, beautiful objects.

40: Be social; be a borrower.

I was shocked when I read in Mai Yururi's *Watashi no uchi niwa nanimo nai* (There's Nothing in My House) that she had thrown away her high school yearbook. I couldn't help thinking that she really must have been true to her nickname, *Sute-hentai* (Weirdo Obsessed with Throwing Things Away) to be able to throw away something irreplaceable like that. But after a while, it occurred to me that since most people usually hang on to their yearbooks, Yururi had simply parted with an item that hundreds of her classmates still had—it wasn't unique or irreplaceable at all.

The desire to hold on to things can also be seen as a desire to avoid troubling someone else for anything. But all this does is shut you off from the world. If you should suddenly have a desperate urge to see your old yearbook, all you have to do is contact one of your old friends and ask them to let you see it. Though you might feel like you're bothering them, in reality they'll probably welcome the chance to spend some time together reminiscing. Anyone who gives you the cold shoulder for a nostalgic request like that isn't really a friend. As long as you remember to express your feelings of gratitude, you aren't going to be a nuisance at all. If anything, your relationships will only deepen.

41: Rent what can be rented.

These days, an amazing array of items can be rented online. If you need to use something only once a year, it might be more practical to just rent it. A lot of long camera lenses are loaned out during the time of year when schools have their field days—think of all those parents scrambling for the right angles to get the best shots of their kids in action. If you don't often take trips abroad, it might be wise to rent your suitcase so you don't have to find a place to keep it tucked away. If you'd like to tidy up important documents that have piled up over the year, you can rent a scanner and turn all that paper into PDF files. You could also rent clothes for the kids to wear for a once-in-a-lifetime event, high-pressure cleaning machines for major tasks, mountain climbing gear or diving equipment, and even flashy outfits that have been styled by a professional.

Why not start by renting something as a trial and then buying it if you really do use it often and you're crazy about it? When you think about the trouble of maintaining most items, rentals are a surprisingly handy and affordable solution.

42: Social media can boost your minimizing motivation.

A helpful trick when going on a weight loss diet is to tell everyone about it. This also works when you're reducing your possessions. It's easy to come up with excuses when you're doing it alone, but we all care about what other people think of us—so why not use that to our advantage? For example, you can use social media to tell people that you're going to cut your clothes collection in half, and make the process public. Share photos of the items you've gotten rid of, or the interior of your closet as it gradually gets cleaned up. Unlike when you're trying to do this alone, you'll get encouragement from your friends, which will boost your motivation.

I also put up pictures of my apartment on my blog, and I think this has helped to further accelerate my minimizing process. There's also a trend among minimalists lately to offer up items they no longer need to people on social media. It helps ease the guilt of throwing things away, and it also makes you feel good knowing that your possessions will be useful to someone else.

43: What if you started from scratch?

In a thought-provoking documentary film called *My Stuff*, the protagonist takes all of his belongings, puts them in storage, and allows himself to retrieve only one item each day. On the first day, he really does have nothing on him; he runs to his storage unit wearing nothing but a newspaper to hide his private parts. He retrieves a coat on the first day and sleeps on the hard floor.

The film was an experiment to see what's really important. Though we might not want to go to the same extreme, we can imagine doing the experiment ourselves. Ask yourself which of your items would truly be necessary if you were to start with zero belongings. What if everything you owned was stolen? What if you had to move next week? Which items would you take with you? There are probably a lot of things we have sitting around in our homes for no particular reason. Think about starting from scratch, and it will become clear which items are essential.

44: Say "see you later" before you say goodbye.

When you aren't sure if you really want to part with something, try stowing it away for a while. A technique that minimalists often use is to gather all the things they're considering getting rid of and place them in a box or in the closet. The trick is to tuck the items away in a place where they do not usually belong. They can even be placed in a garbage bag, so that they are on standby for disposal. Even though they're sitting in a garbage bag, it doesn't mean that you have to actually throw them away quite yet.

A week or a month goes by—the time will depend on the type of items—and if you've managed just fine without them, there's your answer: they aren't necessary for you. If a need arises for some of the items during that period, you don't have to throw those away.

By saying "See you later," you put some distance between you and your possessions, which will allow you to think about their true meaning to you. It's kind of funny how your relationships with your things can be a bit like relationships with people.

45: Discard anything that creates visual noise.

The objects I have at home are white, beige, gray, and the colors of wood, pleasing to the eye and in harmony among themselves. The balance is disrupted when I have something in a flashy neon color or a primary color that's too bold; they stand out too much and disturb the peaceful atmosphere. A jug of bleach, for example, might have a bright pink cap and a mint-colored body. Household cleaning materials are often flashy, which is probably an attempt to warn people of their possible hazards.

Poisonous creatures are generally garish, sending out visual signals to stay away from them. Their bright colors aren't meant to be relaxing. Objects with colors like that enter your field of vision, and hence your awareness, even if you aren't particularly paying attention to them. Small articles adorned with colors are certainly cute. But larger items with bold colors will trigger visual fatigue, and then boredom. You won't tire as quickly of objects that are easier on the eyes and less stimulating, and they can generally be used for longer periods of time.

46: One in, one out.

This is one of the golden rules of minimizing: If you want to buy something, first get rid of something else. Even in the process of minimizing, there will be new items that we need. You can start by getting rid of two or three items when you buy one new item. Once you're down to just your essential possessions, stick with the "one in, one out" rule.

With clothing, you can also predetermine the number of clothes hangers that you have to help you stick to this. You won't be able to increase your clothes collection because you simply won't have anywhere to hang something new.

We should also note that this "one in, one out" rule holds only for items of the same type. For example, if we buy a new jacket, we part with an old jacket. It doesn't make sense to buy a new microwave oven and throw away an old eraser, right?

47: Avoid the Concorde fallacy.

Have you ever heard of the term "Concorde fallacy"? The development of the Concorde, a supersonic jet, is said to have cost about $4 billion. The British and French governments continued to pour money into the project even when it was clear the jet wasn't going to be commercially successful, and it eventually led to about $10 billion in losses. Even when we know that the outlook isn't very bright, it's hard to stop doing something when you consider the time, effort, and costs that have already gone into development.

This happens to us all the time. I bought a hybrid road and mountain bike for only 5,000 yen (about $50), and the purchase prompted an interest in cycling. Then I went out and bought a complete tool kit and began reassembling the components. Guess what happened? I thought about the 5,000 yen purchase I started out with and said to myself, "What's another 10,000 yen [about $100] when I paid so little at the beginning?" I ended up spending more than ten times the initial amount that I paid. Argh. You can also see this effect when we buy those add-ins or upgrades for our smartphone games. We sometimes don't know when to stop, and we end up wasting too much money and time. Watch out for things that can lead to the Concorde fallacy.

48: Be quick to admit mistakes. They help you grow.

We've all done it: we go shopping, buy an outfit that looks good on us in the store, take it home and wear it a few times, and then leave it in the closet. We haven't gotten our money's worth yet so it's hard to throw it away. Or actually, we don't even consider throwing it away. It's still new, after all. Why do we make these shopping mistakes?

Maybe we didn't really love the outfit *that much*, but the shop attendant was very nice. Or it wasn't a perfect fit, but we saw someone else wearing it and it looked great on them. Perhaps it was so cheap, we just had to grab it. Even though the warning signs were already there, we ignored them in favor of the seeming benefits. I still make these types of mistakes.

When we experience shopping mistakes like this, it's better to get rid of the item sooner rather than later. It isn't healthy to spend any more time with an item that signals "failure" to you. Instead, let's try to recognize and learn from our mistakes as soon as we can, so we can make a smarter choice the next time around.

49: Think of buying as renting.

A friend of mine buys a lot of clothes but makes a point of saving all the tags in a bag. He wears his clothes for one season and then he sells them at auction, together with the tags he's saved. With the tags, he can sell his goods at better prices, sometimes for more than he bought them for. He tells me that he considers his clothes "rented from the stores," and when it comes time to "return" them, he sells them to someone else.

I think this is quite an intriguing idea. When you treat the clothes that you buy like they're rented, you handle them with more care. Then you can recycle them in better condition, and you won't be letting anything go to waste. If we think of our purchases as only temporary possessions, it keeps us humble and allows us to better appreciate them.

50: Don't buy it because it's cheap. Don't take it because it's free.

When people buy something worth $50 for $20, they generally think they've saved $30 of their money. It's as if they've actually received $30 by buying that particular product. But we never think about the space we need to store that item in our homes. Let's do a little arithmetic with my rent.

In my case, the monthly rent for my apartment is 67,000 yen (about $650) for twenty square meters, which comes to about 3,000 yen (about $30) per square meter. If the item I bought above for 2,000 yen (about $20) was a one-square-meter dresser, the 3,000 yen I thought I saved would be canceled out right away by the space it took up. It's dangerous to buy something just because it's cheap.

Even something free can be risky. You're bound to be aware of something once you own it, and that alone requires space in our brains. Time and effort will also be needed to manage and care for whatever the item might be. So as it turns out, that "free" item will cost you. Remembering that can help us avoid accumulating too many things just because they happen to be cheap or free.

51: If it's not a "hell, yes!" it's a "no."

When we think about discarding something, sometimes we get stuck weighing its pros and cons. Consider this, though: When we go back and forth like this it's because we think that the two choices have equal value. We're not trying to decide between a gift of $10 or $100, for example—we're deciding between $1 or $1.01.

If that's about the extent of the difference we're facing, we might as well be brave and say goodbye to the item. If you're thinking about reducing the number of things you own, then I recommend discarding something as soon as you start wondering whether or not to do so.

There's a phrase I like that goes, "If it's not a 'hell, yes!' it's a 'no.'" When we ask ourselves, "Should I get rid of this?" we can turn that around: "If it's not a 'hell, no!' it's a 'yes.'" It'll help us discard everything except the things we absolutely can't part with. And we'll be able to manage just fine.

52: The things we really need will always find their way back to us.

Most of us are afraid that if we throw something away, we may never see it again. But we'll never be able to get rid of anything if we start worrying about things like that. Today, we can find almost anything online. A book that's out of print and hard to find at used-book stores can be bought through Amazon.com, and there are auction sites where you can look for the most unique items.

Chances are, you aren't ever going to miss something so much that you become depressed or filled with regret. And if something like that did actually happen, you'd always be able to get hold of it once more. You'll be able to read a book that you want to read again, and someone out there will always have that item that you need to see again. If you miss it so badly that you can't sleep at night, you can always beg its current owner to return it or ask the retailer to send you another one. There are very few things that will become completely out of reach.

53: Keep the gratitude.

We part with items that we've received as gifts. We part with items that used to belong to someone who passed away. We part with items that we can't really make good use of. At those moments, it's the feelings of gratitude we should be embracing.

Someone gave you something, but you don't need it. Though we may not particularly think about it, we will always harbor some type of small resentment about it somewhere in our hearts. But hanging on to that item despite that resentment is disrespectful to the giver and a waste of your energy.

I think it's much more beautiful to focus on your gratitude toward that person as you say a final goodbye to what they gave you. That strong sense of appreciation will remain etched inside us, even after the item is gone, and that's what's really important.

54: Discarding things can be wasteful. But the guilt that keeps you from minimizing is the true waste.

I agree that it's a waste to discard something that can still be used. I don't like simply throwing things into the trash can myself, and I try to let go of my things in such a way that they might be of use to someone else.

The real waste, though, is the psychological damage that you accrue from hanging on to things you don't use or need.

You feel guilty when you look at items that someone gave you as gifts, or that you purchased but never got around to using. They might still be usable, and it would be a waste to throw them away. By keeping these items, though, you guarantee that you'll continue to feel this way today, tomorrow, and beyond. Now, I think that is a true waste.

55: The things we say goodbye to are the things we'll remember forever.

I've scanned every single letter I've received and have thrown away all the originals. Among them, there's something that I'll never be able to forget. It's a train route guide that my mother wrote for me by hand. I left my hometown in Kagawa Prefecture when I enrolled at a university in Tokyo. My mother's guide spelled out which trains to transfer to once I arrived at Haneda Airport so I could get on the monorail train, then the Yamanote Line, then the Seibu Shinjuku Line, and so forth. I don't have a very good sense of direction, and we didn't have smartphones back then. I wonder how my mother felt as she watched me leave for Tokyo?

I'd forgotten that I still had this handwritten train route guide; it had been buried in the mountains of letters that I'd been keeping. It was only when the time came to throw it all away that I realized how valuable it had been to me. As we know, throwing things away does not necessarily mean throwing away our memories. In truth, sometimes the act of saying goodbye is what actually ensures that those memories will remain with us forever.

15 more tips for
the next stage of your
minimalist journey

1: Fewer things does not mean less satisfaction.

The American poet Allen Ginsberg once observed that if you pay twice as much attention to your rug, it'll mean the same thing as owning two rugs. The number of possessions you have has no relevance to the level of satisfaction that you'll get from them.

It's said that having a possession is knowing that you own something and having a strong awareness of that ownership. That's the way our brains function. To be acutely aware of a small group of cherished possessions, rather than having a haphazard awareness of a large pile of adequate possessions, can double or triple the satisfaction we get from our things.

We feel greater satisfaction when we own and treasure one irreplaceable coffee cup than we do when we have two or three mugs that we aren't particularly crazy about. Reducing the number of items that we own does not reduce our satisfaction.

2: Find your unique uniform.

Steve Jobs always wore the same clothes: a black turtleneck by Issey Miyake, Levi's 501s, and a pair of New Balance sneakers, which even served as his attire for public presentations. Facebook founder Mark Zuckerberg seems to be fond of a gray T-shirt. Einstein is said to have always worn the same type of jacket. These people took the time that others spend on choosing clothes and chasing trends and turned their attention instead to the things that mattered most to them.

We don't need to have a lot of clothes to live a clean, comfortable life. While others may like to vary their looks, there's a stylishness to wearing the same clothes that are perfect for us and using them as a kind of personal uniform.

Though some people might judge you if you're always wearing the same style, I think that will eventually become a thing of the past. I agree that fashion can be fun, but chasing trends can get excessive in today's world.

3: We find our originality when we own less.

What do you think makes someone unique? Is it having bright green streaks in their hair, or wearing a huge ring through their lip? Is a man wearing a skirt unique? Or maybe it's just someone with an edgy, oversized case for their smartphone?

I think being truly original has nothing to do with any of these things. All the minimalists I've met to date have been uniquely individual and pretty cool, even if they were wearing very orthodox clothing as their personal uniform.

Although it may seem like you're losing your individuality when you part with your belongings, the reality seems to be the other way around. Take the people you see in old European photographs as an example. All the men are generally wearing the same types of suits and hats, and they're all smoking cigarettes with the same sort of possessions around them. Yet the art and literature that those people created was incredibly original, to say the least.

When you think about it, it's experience that builds our unique characteristics, not material objects. So maybe it's natural that we find our own originality when we strip away all the things that distract us.

4: Discard it if you've thought about doing so five times.

We humans think roughly sixty thousand thoughts in a single day. I've tried tracking my thoughts and found that they really do go flying about in every direction.

Maybe there's a cup sitting on the table in front of me after I've had my coffee. I can still taste the coffee in my mouth. I touch my lips, I want to brush my teeth—that's right, I need to buy a new toothbrush. And speaking of toothbrushes, there was this thing that happened the other day . . . and so forth.

In this way, our awareness is an endless chain of thoughts. A single thought out of the sixty thousand that come to mind in a day will, quite naturally, go by unnoticed.

Even if you haven't arrived at a concrete decision to discard something, chances are you've probably thought about it briefly when you glance at the item. If those casual glances have occurred five times, it means you're ready to part with that item. Those five passing thoughts will soon multiply to a hundred and then a thousand if you don't act.

5: If you've developed your minimalist skills, you can skip the "see you later" stage.

Consider this an upgraded version of tip 44, for those of you well on your way to a minimalist lifestyle. If you can't make up your mind about an item, I suggest you go right ahead and discard it. One of the very last things I discarded was my TV, and when I did I still had concerns. I thought it might cause issues in my line of work if I became unfamiliar with current events. It might make me an outcast among my friends if I couldn't keep up with their discussions. Maybe even little kids would start making fun of me if I didn't have a clue about the latest comedy acts. I reminded myself that if I needed to, I could go running to the store to buy a new TV. But you know what? Nothing like that happened.

There's only one item that I bought again after letting it go. It's a foot massager from the manufacturer Omron. I love it so much I even memorized the model number. I bought one as a gift for my mother, and I gave my brother the one that I had been using. But as it turned out, I couldn't forget how good it felt to have my feet massaged by that little device, so I went out and bought it again. Then later, I felt I was ready to part with it again and went ahead and sold it. I'll probably hang on to it forever if I end up buying it a third time.

6: A little inconvenience can make us happier.

I recently got rid of all the towels I have at home and switched to a single *tenugui*, a thin Japanese hand towel. It's amazing. It can be used in many ways, and you'd be shocked by how quickly it dries. I use it, leave it hanging, and it's dry the next time I need it. I use it to wash my hands, do the dishes, and dry my body after taking a shower. All my old towels used to make up about two-thirds of my laundry. Without all those soft and fluffy—but also bulky—towels, doing the laundry has become much easier.

As I explained in chapter 2, people tend to see variances as stimulation, so the fluffy towels that we use each day have become things we take for granted. Sure, an oversized bath towel will feel much nicer than a hand towel. But in the same way that we get used to such conveniences, we also get used to inconveniences. When a *tenugui* becomes a daily item, the rare use of a real towel gives me a lot of pleasure. I've lowered my bar for happiness simply by switching to a *tenugui*. When even a regular bath towel can make you happy, you'll be able to find happiness almost anywhere.

7: Discard it even if it sparks joy.

If you've decided to become a minimalist, there will come a time when you have to part with an item or two that sparks joy. For me, I have a deep affection for Croatia, and a cross that I bought during a visit there was definitely something that made my heart dance. It was a ceramic cross in a scarlet color, adorned with an intricate design crafted by hand. The colors, the smooth texture, the comfortable weight—I loved everything about it. I was told that it had been made by a local artist, and more than anything, the sense of coming across it on a street in a foreign country and not at a souvenir shop made it all the more precious to me.

The cross was something that sparked my joy, even when I parted with it. Still, I'm really glad I worked up the courage to say goodbye to it. Since then, I no longer spend time looking for souvenirs when I travel. I follow the example of Snufkin—one of the characters from Tove Jansson's *Moomin*—and only *look* at souvenirs, no matter how tempting they are. This has allowed me to focus more on the journey itself. And what is life if not a journey? Be brave and let go of things that spark joy—what you gain can be tremendous.

8: Minimalism is freedom—the sooner you experience it, the better.

Most of our possessions are things that have value only to us: souvenirs from memorable trips, beloved books we've read over and over, letters we received from people important to us, and photographs of unforgettable moments.

The memories of the trouble we went through to obtain a certain object, the price we paid to make it our own, or the stories that surround it will raise its value to us. But no matter how expensive or how wonderful an item may be to us, it won't have that same value to someone else. It will simply be another item.

This thought crossed my mind when I was thinking about what would happen if I passed away, or something serious happened to me suddenly. All my possessions would become a burden to my loved ones. Yet because I had minimized most of my belongings, I realized I had also minimized the trouble I would cause others in such circumstances. It's a sad thing to think about, but for some reason I felt a sense of freedom. Without such a morose concern hanging over me, I felt stronger and free to tackle the next stage of my life.

9: Discarding things may leave you with less, but it will never make you a lesser person.

If you decide to minimize your possessions, you won't suddenly develop a mysterious rash, have half your hair turn gray overnight, or develop arthritis. It won't become obvious to passersby, you won't be criticized for it, and you won't have little kids throwing rocks at you. Maybe they'll just look at you and think you're dressed in a simple style. That's about all there is to it.

When you're surrounded by a lot of things, getting rid of your cherished items may seem like you're tearing away pieces of yourself. But remember, those things aren't you; your close connection to them is entirely a creation in your mind. You won't become less of a person by doing away with those things. In fact, you may actually be pleasantly surprised to find that with all those extraneous possessions out of the way, the true you will begin to come alive.

10: Question the conventional ways you're expected to use things.

Hiji is one of the minimalists featured at the beginning of this book. The sofa he came up with is a folded mattress placed against a wall that uses his pillow and comforter as a backrest. It's an example of reverse thinking: not a "sofa bed" but a "bed sofa" (or "mattress sofa," to be more precise). As long as you have a recorder and a head-mounted viewer, you can watch TV shows without a TV set. You can also use body soap as laundry detergent or for washing the dishes.

I've recently started hanging my sponge out to dry, influenced by Marie Kondo, who says she hang-dries all kinds of things, including her cutting board and dishwashing sponge. This has enabled me to get rid of the sponge dish with the suction cups that I hated. Kondo went beyond the common sense that cutting boards and sponges didn't belong on a laundry line. Our possessions will keep increasing if we're constrained by the standard uses or conveniences of each item, but we can de-clutter surprisingly well if we ignore convention.

11: Don't think. Discard!

One of Bruce Lee's famous lines from *Enter the Dragon* is "Don't think. Feel." To apply this to minimalists, the line would probably go, "Don't think. Discard!"

There was a day when I suddenly got sick and tired of having so many important-looking bankbooks* at home and threw them all into the shredder.

I figured I'd manage somehow, so I went ahead and did it, and then afterward I went to Yahoo Answers and asked, "Is it okay to throw away a bankbook?" Rather than think about it, I followed my instinct.

Later on, I took the necessary steps to close the account and had no problem whatsoever. The bank teller was just a little stunned when I explained what I had done.

"You . . . discarded . . . your bankbook?"

But there are people who lose everything in a fire, so it can't be that big a deal to throw a few things away. The more we think about it, the more our brains will keep coming up with excuses why we can't part with our belongings. When that happens? Trust your instincts.

---

* Pocket-sized books of official transaction records for your bank account.

12: Minimalism is not a competition. Don't boast about how little you have. Don't judge someone who has more than you.

A minimalist can easily fall into the trap of bragging about how little they have or competing with others over who has the least. As I said in chapter 1, I think a minimalist is a person who knows what's truly necessary for them, a person who reduces so they can focus on what's really important. The things that are necessary will vary from person to person, so there isn't much point to comparing yourself with others.

In my opinion, a person can be surrounded with a lot of possessions that are truly necessary to them. If owning many things gives someone real meaning and purpose, then there's really no need for them to try to get rid of anything. There's no reason to judge a person like that.

Similarly, there's no need to go too far and part with things that are really necessary for you. Minimalism is not a rite of penance, nor is it a competitive sport. It is simply a means to an end.

13: The desire to discard and the desire to possess are flip sides of the same coin.

It can be pretty stimulating when you start getting rid of your possessions. It's refreshing, and the rewards for finding the courage to let go of things are immediately visible. Once you fall under the spell of this minimizing process, parting with your possessions becomes a supreme directive, so much so that it's almost like you've contracted "get-rid-of-everything" disease. You feel proud of your achievement, and then you start feeling critical about people who have a lot of stuff.

But that judgment of "Ugh, you still own so much. How lame!" is exactly the same mind-set as "Ugh, you still don't have this. How lame!"

There's stimulation in both discarding and obtaining alike, so we shouldn't become too dependent on either type of action. We know that when you decide to discard something you should ask yourself, "Is this something that I really need?" In the same way, it's also necessary to ask ourselves, "Is this something that I should really get rid of? Am I trying to discard it for the sole purpose of reducing everything I have?"

14: Find your own minimalism.

Maybe you don't think you qualify as a minimalist unless all your possessions fit into a single suitcase, or you sleep in a sleeping bag. But rest assured, there are no such requirements. There is no single correct definition of a minimalist. Maybe after you've parted with a lot of your possessions, a big piano remains sitting in your home. As a result of reducing a lot of your belongings, you've become aware of what's truly necessary and important to you: music.

Mr. Numahata, the person I run a website with, has bought a car, saying that's where minimalism has led him. He has reduced his unnecessary interpersonal relationships, and his car helps him make the time to be alone. He can also keep the interior completely free of possessions, and consider it a minimalist room that's mobile. Feel free to experiment and find your own minimalism.

15: Minimalism is a method and a beginning.

I've mentioned some of the traps that minimalists may fall into, but I would like to say here that minimalism is still something that I would recommend to nearly everyone. Society today puts too much weight on material objects, and there are too many people who own way more than they need.

For a minimalist, the objective isn't to reduce, it's to eliminate distractions so they can focus on the things that are truly important. Minimalism is just the beginning. It's a tool. Once you've gone ahead and minimized, it's time to find out what those important things are.

Minimalism is like the prologue of a book; the stories to follow can only be created by the individual. As I've said, minimalism is so effective and its methods so worthwhile that people can get confused and think it's their true objective. But remember, the important thing is what you're going to do after. Once you've said goodbye to all those extra things, it's time to create your own unique story.

4

12 ways I've changed since I said goodbye to my things

I have more time.

*Your time is limited, so don't waste it
living someone else's life.*

—STEVE JOBS

How possessions take your time

On December 20, 2014, special limited-edition Suica fare cards were issued to commemorate Tokyo Station's hundredth year in service. Fifteen thousand cards were made available for sale, and the result was bedlam. More than nine thousand people got in line to buy the Suica cards, and sales had to be suspended on that day.

Television news segments showed the reactions of angry people after sales had been suspended, including children who had been waiting in line so they could obtain the Suica cards to use when they started attending junior high school the following spring. I felt sincerely sorry for all those people who waited in line for hours in the cold weather.

But it isn't as if those limited-edition Suica cards offered a 5 percent discount on train fare or used a special material that didn't easily break. I would certainly want one if they did. The Mucha-esque design is definitely beautiful, but I wonder if this card was something that everyone simply *wanted*, not so much as *needed*?

If you decided that the functions of the limited-edition cards were exactly the same as the usual cards and ignored them, look at how much time you saved:

1. The time spent getting to and from Tokyo Station
2. The time spent waiting in line
3. The time lost simply feeling angry after being told that sales have been canceled

4. The time spent controlling your anger
5. The time spent figuring out what to do next and maybe even planning your next attempt to purchase the card

Listen, life is short. It's a shame to waste it because of some material object.

Less time spent being distracted by the media or by ads

Whether sitting at home watching TV or stepping outside, we're bombarded by urgent messages through the media, ads, and everything else that we come across.

Let's make as much money as we can and build our savings. Let's trim that fat and become slim. Let's get into a good school. Let's live in a nice house. Let's get healthy. Let's compete and win. Let's be more stylish. Let's acquire more knowledge. Let's prepare for disaster.

The film director Tom Shadyac said simply, "In other words, we're no good as we are."

When we practice minimalism, we'll spend less time being distracted by the media or by advertisements because we become aware that we already have everything that we need. And when we feel this way, we can easily ignore most of these messages that cry out to us.

Conversely, if we're constantly thinking that we're missing something in our lives, we'll feel as if all those messages are directed straight at us. If we start to contemplate every one of those messages, we'll never have enough time to do anything. Minimalism is built around the idea that there's nothing that you're lacking. You'll spend less time being pushed around by something that you think you may be missing.

Less time spent shopping

A minimalist doesn't buy much to begin with so you will spend less time shopping. Though there are bound to be things you need to purchase, it'll take less time to get them. Back in my maximalist days, I used to be a big fan of electric appliances. Let's say I wanted to buy a new microwave oven. I would go through the product specifications from different manufacturers with a fine-tooth comb. I'd check all the user reviews on the web. I'd make a comprehensive evaluation and buy a model that allowed me to steam cook at high temperatures. I'd be overjoyed with some feature that wasn't available in other models from the same price range—and then never once use that feature when cooking.

I would stop by a chic area of Tokyo and spend a whole day looking for the perfect shirt. Sometimes I'd go from store A to B and on to C, try on different shirts but be unable to decide, go back to store A again but still come back empty-handed. What was the point of my day spent shopping? Did I just go to tire myself out?

There's a famous study called the Jam Study. In short, more

people purchased jam when six varieties were displayed than when twenty-four varieties were available. When given too many choices, people tend to worry that there's something better out there than what they decided on. If they buy one of the varieties, their satisfaction level will actually decrease because of this feeling of regret. It gets complicated when there are too many choices available.

As I continue in my journey as a minimalist, I've noticed that my criteria for choosing things has become clearer, and as a result, I spend less time wondering whether or not to buy something. The qualities I look for in the things I buy are (1) the item has a minimalist type of shape, and is easy to clean; (2) its color isn't too loud; (3) I'll be able to use it for a long time; (4) it has a simple structure; (5) it's lightweight and compact; and (6) it has multiple uses.

My choice of a bicycle then became simple. I looked for a fixed-gear bike with a plain silver, raw finish, the kind of color that looks slightly rusty to begin with. A classic horizontal frame that wouldn't go out of style. I didn't need the name of a fancy brand on the frame. The only bicycle that met my criteria was one sold by Focale 44, so it took no time to decide. Once I did, I didn't compare it with other bikes, either.

No time is wasted pondering choices if you continue to buy the same product that you like or if you keep repairing it as needed. And since you're satisfied with it, you don't need to worry about glancing at other new models. This doesn't just apply to products. Minimalism naturally narrows down your choices so you can arrive at quick decisions.

Less time spent doing chores

I've experienced a drastic reduction in time spent doing my housework.

I'll go into detail later but it's amazing how cleaning time is reduced when you keep things minimal. You'll have fewer things to leave lying around. Own fewer clothes and you'll be doing less laundry, and you'll also be wasting less time trying to decide what to wear.

I used to hate the rays of the sun in my messy old apartment. I hated the dust that would be highlighted by the sunlight. I was a night person, and the sliding shutters on my window were always closed to keep the sun out.

But now I awaken as the sun shines into my home. I wake up, see that my room is already clean, and it's become something of a joy just getting up in the morning. I wake up early without any effort. The morning hours that used to be nonexistent for me are now filled with meaning.

I can move out of my home in thirty minutes

This spring, I moved into a new apartment. I didn't do any packing beforehand and yet it only took thirty minutes to take everything out of my home, including the time it took to remove the light fixtures and unplug the washing machine. That's how long it might take a person who needs time to decide what to wear before they leave their home. But in my minimalist style, I no longer need a lot of time to pack up my possessions. I'm able to move anywhere I like with the same casualness as stepping out for coffee.

Less time spent lazing around

When you live in a home that's clean and simple, you spend less time lazing around. Back in my old apartment I used to stay in bed all day when I had time off from work. I might think, *I have to do the laundry today. And it's about time I vacuumed the place, too. But wait, how long has it been since I last washed these sheets? Okay, I'll get to it . . . but where should I start? I'll do the laundry, clean, and do the dishes while the washing machine is in full action. Yeah, that's what I'll do. But wait, maybe I should clean while wearing these clothes and throw them in the washing machine after I'm done. Oh, it's so much trouble . . . I'll just turn on the TV and check my smartphone first. . . .* This is an endless loop. But when you have few possessions, there are fewer things that need to be done each day. You can take care of each task as it arises, so you don't end up with a long list of things to do, which leaves you with a lively spirit and drive.

Less time spent looking for missing items

I'm aware of every single one of my possessions, and since they're always stored in the same location, I spend zero minutes looking for misplaced things. When you're aware of all the things that you own, you're not only certain of where they are, you're also sure about whether you have them or not. There's no need to waste time asking yourself where you put the packing tape. I don't keep a roll of packing tape in my home, so my answer is obvious. Instructions on how to use products, warranty cards, documents—I scan all of these immediately or simply throw them away. If the need arises for any of these documents, I know I don't have to go searching for the hard copy.

With fewer possessions, you will have fewer things to lose. And since a minimalist also usually goes out with fewer possessions, the chances of forgetting something decrease, which also means less time running home to fetch something that was left behind.

Quality time, not quality objects, leads to happiness

I often see people running frantically to jump on a train, almost bumping into people in the process. Every time I see a person like that, I can't help but notice that he or she does not look happy. No one's beaming with joy when they're rushed. On the other hand, the people I see on the streets during Japan's Golden Week holidays look considerably happier.

Psychologist Tim Kasser stresses that the enrichment of time will lead directly to happiness, while the enrichment of material objects will not. We all know people who are great at their jobs and make a lot of money but are always stressed out, going from one crisis to another. Even pleasant people will turn negative if they're too busy and don't have the luxury of time on their hands.

The importance of daydreaming

Recent studies in neuroscience have revealed that there are certain areas in our brain that are active only when we're daydreaming or when our minds are wandering.

These moments are said to be used for self-awareness, orientation, and memory—or to put it simply, to think about ourselves. A relaxed moment is not without meaning; it's an important time for reflection. Maybe we're sitting at a beach and listening to the sounds of the waves or gazing into a campfire.

Science has proven that these types of relaxed intervals are necessary for us. Whether we're rich or poor, we all get twenty-four hours in a day. Finding time to relax is the ultimate luxury.

You can feel happy right now

Experiencing relaxation is indispensable for feeling happiness. But that doesn't mean you need to take a vacation to a tropical island and lie on a beach chair under an umbrella. There actually isn't much emotional difference between the everyday happiness within your grasp right now and the happiness you'll find at that beach. Take a breather at a neighborhood coffee shop. Stop typing away at your computer and give yourself a moment to take a deep breath. Happiness is actually all around us. We just need time to find it.

By reducing the number of material possessions you have, you can take back the time that your belongings have been stealing from you. That time is precious. It's a shame to waste away what is allocated equally to all of us—only twenty-four hours a day—on material belongings. Instead, devote that time to the pursuit of everyday happiness.

I enjoy life more.

My life itself was become my amusement and never ceased to be novel. It was a drama of many scenes and without an end.

—HENRY DAVID THOREAU

Everyone likes the results of a good housecleaning

Though most of us aren't excited by the idea of cleaning house, there's probably not a single person who doesn't like the *results* of a good cleaning. Would anyone look at a room that's been thoroughly cleaned and curse? I don't think so. A spotless room is a welcoming sight for anyone.

Back when I was surrounded by stuff, I used to hate cleaning. No matter how often I cleaned, dust would keep accumulating. I also hated doing the dishes. I'd look at them all piled up in my kitchen sink and promise myself that I would get to them tomorrow. Then I'd head straight to bed.

I hated this never-ending cycle of housework. Unsurprisingly, my home was always a mess. There even came a time when all the floor space was filled with books and I recall thinking that at least I would no longer need to clean the place.

Near my old apartment, there was a gingko tree that loomed over the sidewalk. Each morning, I would see my middle-aged neighbor busy sweeping away the fallen leaves and wonder how she could stand doing that day after day. The leaves were falling all the time anyway, so why didn't she just take care of the sweeping once a week or even every other day?

That had been the old me. Now I can understand how the woman must have felt. It wasn't the fallen leaves that she had been tidying up; it was her own laziness that she had been sweeping away.

There's no such thing as a lazy personality

I used to think of myself as a lazy person with no willpower. I believed it was a personality trait that couldn't be changed. And besides, I would tell myself, how unusual was it for a guy to be a slob, anyway?

But all that has now changed. Each morning, I vacuum my apartment before heading off to work. I tidy up the bathroom whenever I take a shower, and as a result it's always squeaky-clean and shining. I do the dishes as soon as I finish eating. I do the laundry before my dirty clothes form a huge pile and hang dry the washed items on my balcony, where I also wipe everything down, including my neighbor's balcony.

Yet I haven't gone through a personality change. So why am I no longer a "lazy slob"? The simple reason for the clean new me is that I now have fewer possessions and it's simply easier to clean house. I don't have a lazy personality now, and I didn't back then.

Aristotle's method for cleaning up

Aristotle believed (as paraphrased by philosopher Will Durant) that "We are what we repeatedly do. Excellence, then, is not an act but a habit." You don't need a strong will to tidy up regularly and maintain a clean home. Determination alone will eventually fade anyway. All you need to do is to make household cleanup a daily habit. Once it becomes a habit, you'll be able to clean up without a second thought.

The rewards for making cleanup a habit

It's said that getting a reward is key to developing a new habit. With daily cleaning, the reward may be the sense of accomplishment and calmness we feel afterward. There's also the reward of the self-confidence we gain when we've overcome all those excuses for not tidying up. As minimalists, cleaning becomes easy and quick, yet we still get rewarded all the same. We actually start to enjoy cleaning as a result, and it naturally becomes a habit. Same goes for all the other chores that need to be done at home. To develop a cleaning habit, the important thing is to make it easy to get those rewards. It'll be a snap if you have fewer possessions.

Cleaning becomes three times easier when you have less

When I had been living in my old apartment, I might have vacuumed once in a good month. Even after I had minimized quite a bit, I still only cleaned my apartment on the weekends. But now I vacuum my new apartment every morning. It became a habit simply because it's so easy.

Cleaning can be really easy if you have fewer things. Let's

look at how we might clean the floor if we had an owl sculpture in the room.

Step 1: Move the owl over.

Step 2: Wipe the floor where the owl had been sitting.

Step 3: Return the owl to its original position.

And if we didn't have this statue in our home?

Step 1: Wipe the floor.

There! Done! It's that simple. It takes a third of the effort, and probably a third of the time, to clean the floor. And forget about wiping those intricate hollows and crevices in the sculpture itself.

Now imagine the work we'd have to do if we owned three or four, or maybe ten or twenty of these sculptures at home.

Without clutter, your possessions have a natural resting place

Now that I've discovered the comfort of living in a place that isn't cluttered with objects, I've become quick to put things away. I put my hair dryer away as soon as I finish using it. There had once been a time when I couldn't believe it when Marie Kondo said she only pulls out her remote control for the TV when she wants to use it, but I'm finding now that I'm doing the same thing. It's really no trouble at all. Once it becomes a habit, it's a natural flow to bring something out, use it, and then put it away again.

Remember when you first learned to ride a bicycle? I'm sure you must have been very careful to maintain your balance as you pedaled. But the skill is soon acquired and before you know it, you're riding without a second thought.

It's the same way when I clean house. I don't really think about it; it's as if my possessions return to their rightful positions on their own.

The joys of living in a small apartment

This spring, I moved from a twenty-five-square-meter (about three hundred square feet) home to a smaller place that's twenty square meters in size. What this means is that I now have five square meters less space that needs to be cleaned. Housecleaning is easier than ever, not to mention quicker.

My feeling now is that I would like to live in as small a place as possible. Even my current apartment was a bit too spacious for me at first. The cleaning work is simple, fun, and it feels good. I doubt I'll ever buy a robot vacuum cleaner or have someone else do the cleaning for me when it can be such an enjoyable task. And in my small apartment, with my few cherished possessions, cleaning really becomes an intimate act as well.

Dust and grime are reflections of our past selves

It's often said that cleaning your house is like polishing yourself. I think that this is a golden rule. It isn't just dust and dirt that accumulate in our homes. It's also the shadows of our past selves that let that dust and dirt continue to build. Cleaning the grime is certainly unpleasant, but more than that, it's the need to face our own past deeds that makes it so tough. But when we have fewer material possessions and cleaning becomes an easy habit, the shadows we now face will be of our daily accomplishments.

Getting up early in the morning, taking a refreshing shower, sitting down to a leisurely breakfast, cleaning, and doing the laundry before you leave for work will definitely affect the way you get on at the office. Simply by living an organized life, you'll be more invigorated, more confident, and like yourself better compared with when you used to stay in bed until the last minute and rush through everything just to get to work. And when you like yourself, it'll be easier to take on other challenges. People can change, starting with their lifestyles.

The pressure to build a "successful" future

"You're important, and you're irreplaceable."
"Be yourself, and be unique."
"Go for it. Strive to achieve something."

We know everyone means well, but young people are probably bombarded with these types of messages on a daily basis. They're constantly being pressured to become someone. I, too, had been under the same kind of pressure, and I was frustrated by my inability to fulfill these expectations.

Having parted with most of my belongings, one thing that I can honestly say now is that there isn't really a need to accomplish something or build an ambitious future. We can begin to be content with ourselves and feel plenty of happiness by simply going about our daily lives, appreciating the present moment.

When I finish my simple cleaning tasks in my new apartment and take a stroll around the neighborhood, I realize there isn't anything more that I need or want. I go to the park and watch the ducks in the pond as they fluff their feathers. I see how relaxed they look—when all they're doing is fluffing their feathers. They aren't filled with tension trying to become something else. They aren't frantically attempting to build their careers, and they aren't sucking up to the other ducks. All they seem to be doing is enjoying the water, fluffing their feathers, and living their lives. When it comes right down to it, isn't that all we really need in our lives, too?

Having parted with the bulk of my belongings, I feel true contentment with my day-to-day life. The very act of living brings me joy.

I have more freedom.

It's only after we've lost everything that we're free to do anything.

—TYLER DURDEN, *FIGHT CLUB*

The freedom to move

Isn't it true that birds are free to soar high into the sky because their nests are simple and they aren't weighed down by the need to accumulate things?

I used to be the complete opposite of those birds. I had a huge shelving unit taking up space in the kitchen, and at one point I even had a darkroom set up in one corner of my place. In the hallway stood massive bookshelves holding tons of books. I used to think back then that for my next move I would need lots of space and storage for all these things, and probably even a whole extra room where my huge TV set and home theater setup could be fully enjoyed. I would look for available apartments on the web but could never find such a place within my budget. And besides, it was going to be a pain in the neck packing up all those things and then unpacking them again at my new place.

After going minimalist, I moved for the first time in a decade. It was from Nakameguro to an area called Fudomae, not too far away, and the packing (without a single cardboard box, mind you), the move itself, and unpacking all took but an hour and a half. I kid you not. The next time I move, I'd like to find an even smaller place to live. The twenty-square-meter apartment where I now live seems to be too large for me. It would be lovely to live in a place of about twelve square meters (about one hundred thirty square feet) like author Dominique

Loreau. Plus, with smaller apartments comes lower rent. I've finally been freed from all my old search criteria—a need for so much space to store this item or that, and a living room that has to be so many square meters big to put everything in it. It takes so little time to move to a new place. I've parted with my possessions and gained the freedom to move whenever the mood strikes.

The freedom to choose a new lifestyle

Many people are now exploring various new types of housing. Some examples are author Tomoya Takamura's hut that he built for $1,000, Kyohei Sakaguchi's mobile house, and of course the tiny house movement. These initiatives are all creative alternatives to the conventional thirty-year mortgage.

The number of vacant houses in Japan is expected by some accounts to reach 40 percent by the year 2040. Plus, with Japan's frequent earthquakes, the risks of living in a conventional home continue to increase each year. All these new lifestyle options have one thing in common: they are not normal, large houses where many things can be stored.

It's easy for a minimalist who has few possessions to choose any type of home they desire, and I find all these new lifestyle options fascinating. I imagine the trend will continue to gain momentum.

Lower living costs lead to a freer life

There's an important concept called *minimum living costs*, that refers to the minimum amount of money you need to live. I think it's worthwhile for everyone to calculate this for themselves at least once, by adding up rent, groceries, utilities, communication charges, and so on.

I live in a place called Fudomae in Tokyo and my monthly rent is 67,000 yen (about $650). I can live happily on 100,000 yen (about $1,000) a month, and that includes other modern necessities like my iPhone. I'm perfectly happy cooking all my meals, doing my reading at the library, and taking walks in the park to relax.

It's all possible, even enjoyable, because when you take up minimalism you really do stop comparing yourself with others. And once you let go of the needless pride that triggers thoughts like, "I'm not someone who should be doing this kind of work!" or "I'd like to live in a home like they featured in that magazine," or "I don't want people to think I'm poor," there are plenty of jobs out there that'll pay 100,000 yen a month.

As a result, I don't even have to worry about retirement anymore. I'm optimistic, knowing that all I have to do is earn 100,000 yen each month. Many jobs are available today where all you need is an online connection, so you can even live someplace abroad where minimum living costs are even lower. There's no point in putting up with a terrible job or working yourself to death just to maintain your standard of living. By having less and lowering your minimum living costs, you can go anywhere you want. Minimalism can really be liberating.

Liberated from your personas

We all identify with our possessions to some extent. I considered my huge collection of books, CDs, and DVDs as a part of who I was. It's hard to part with something that you love, because it makes you feel as if you're throwing a part of yourself away, and I can certainly relate to that. But the truth is, by letting go of my books, CDs, and DVDs, I was able to achieve a fundamental sense of freedom that's hard to put into words—it's freedom from my personas, you could say.

As a self-proclaimed connoisseur of film, I used to watch five or six movies a week. I would be embarrassed if there was a movie that everyone was talking about that I hadn't seen; I wanted to show off the fact that I saw so many movies. I wanted to be able to say, "That movie? Yeah, I saw it. I saw that other one, too. Yeah, I'd like to even see this other movie, too." Though I still remain a fan of movies, I realize that before, I was just attached to this persona of a "film enthusiast." These days, I don't worry about how many movies I see. I'm no longer a "film enthusiast," but someone instead who enjoys only the movies I really need to see.

Now when an unfamiliar film title comes up in conversation, I have no qualms about asking, "What's that? Tell me about it."

There are things you love so much that they start to feel like they're a part of you. They assemble themselves into a persona that you then have to maintain. Parting with those things means you're freeing yourself from that particular consciousness.

Liberated from greed

When you become a minimalist, you free yourself from all the materialist messages that surround us. All the creative marketing and annoying advertisements no longer have an effect on you. Celebrities no longer make you feel envious. Fancy window displays, reward cards, spiffy new high-spec products, new high-rise condos under construction—none of it has anything to do with you, and you can stroll around town feeling comfortable and free.

As I explained in chapter 2, the more things you have, the more you accumulate. You'll never be satisfied when trapped in this cycle; it will only make you want more and more.

It's like a monster that becomes hungrier and hungrier as it eats. *Wetiko* is a Native American word, literally translated as "man-eater," which refers to a mental disorder in which you want more than you need. This disorder destroys people's lives.

Left to its own devices, our hunger for things can grow out of control and become a monster. In the past, I was overwhelmed by greed. I was always looking for more. But now I have everything I need.

There's nothing in particular I really want. It may come as a surprise, but it's really a fantastic feeling.

I no longer compare myself with others.

When you realize there is nothing lacking,
the whole world belongs to you.

—LAO TZU

How to become instantly unhappy

Want to know how to make yourself instantly unhappy? Compare yourself with someone else.

I once watched a girl I used to love marry a guy who made a lot of money. I compared myself with him and felt miserable, blaming my income for losing her. But thinking about it now, money wasn't what I was lacking.

When you compare yourself with successful people your age, you can't help but feel foolish and incompetent. Social media can seem full of people who are enjoying their life more than you. You can be walking down the street, see a group of strangers having fun, and immediately feel lonely.

We always think the grass is greener next door. But the grass itself doesn't care. It's the person who owns that grass who's concerned about it. Sometimes we even use chemicals to dye the grass green so it matches the neighbor's lawn. But at some point, that grass is going to turn brown, its natural beauty destroyed because of needless comparison.

Who does Bill Gates compare himself with?

We can't help comparing ourselves with others. The problem is that there's no end to these comparisons.

Let's say there's a guy who works at a tech start-up. He'll

see a very skilled senior member of the company and compare himself with her. In turn, that woman might be comparing herself with the CEO who started the company, while the CEO may be comparing himself with another CEO of a bigger, more successful company, and that CEO will be comparing herself with Bill Gates. So, who does Bill Gates compare himself with? Maybe it's the younger version of himself, or a soon-to-be-famous young entrepreneur.

Once you start comparing yourself with others, you're always going to find someone who's better than you. No matter how rich you might be, how handsome, or how beautiful, there's always going to be another person who's richer or more beautiful. Even if you became a member of a big pop group in Japan, you might still feel miserable when you compare yourself with Johnny Depp or Brad Pitt. Or maybe you've realized your childhood dream of becoming a soccer player, yet you're still unhappy because you keep comparing yourself with Lionel Messi. Even if you rise to the top in a certain field, you'll always find ways to compare yourself with people in other fields.

Now that I have parted with my possessions, I no longer compare myself with anyone. I used to be embarrassed whenever I compared my miserable apartment with someone else's home. Or I would see an acquaintance buying everything they wanted and feel envious. But now I've been able to say goodbye to that old me, because I've stopped taking part in that rat race of never-ending comparison and accumulation.

Experiences resist comparison

As I explained in chapter 2, people get used to objects. And it's known that happiness continues for longer periods if it's based on experiences rather than objects. A $1,000 coat will lose its novelty as you continue to wear it, but if you had spent the money on a trip with a friend, you can relive that joy every time you remember that trip. And the joy doesn't fade when you revisit it.

So why do we tend to spend money on things instead of experiences? It goes back to our need to compare ourselves with others. Psychologist Sonja Lyubomirsky points out that it's easy to compare your handbag with other people's handbags, since the price tag makes the value of a bag obvious. If it's a designer bag, then it's even easier to compare, because everyone is immediately aware of its value.

On the other hand, a considerable amount of imagination is necessary if you want to compare your yoga class to someone else's game of golf, or your fishing trip to another person's camping expedition.

Perhaps that's why experiences give you longer periods of happiness. You'll feel a much richer sense of contentment by building your experiences rather than buying items, because your experiences resist comparison with others'. And because they are tough to compare, your experiences don't even have to be anything rare or expensive to be special to you.

When you stop comparing, you find yourself

Just like our accumulation of material objects, once we start comparing ourselves with others, it will be endless. In the process of writing this book, I would never have been able to write a single word if I had started thinking about books that have been written by people who are better than I am. Let's face it, there will always be people who are better than we are. If we start comparing ourselves with those people, agonizing over how we think we're nothing compared with them, we'll be completely paralyzed.

But when you say goodbye to all your unnecessary things, you also say goodbye to the process of comparing yourself with other people. After all, you no longer have any of those material objects that are used to compare your status with others'.

And once you are a minimalist who only has what *you* need, your focus will inevitably shift from others to yourself. Freed from comparing, you'll start to discover who you truly are.

I stopped worrying about
how others see me.

You're the only one who's worried about your face.

—ICHIRO KISHIMI AND FUMITAKE KOGA,
KIRAWARERU YUKI (COURAGE TO BE DISLIKED)

Steve Jobs didn't get nervous

In the process of minimizing, I went through my clothes and minimized my wardrobe as well. As I explained in chapter 3, it's possible to create more time and focus on the important things if we consider personal uniforms. Steve Jobs had his black turtleneck, and Mark Zuckerberg has his gray T-shirt. They agreed that it's a waste of time selecting which clothes you want to wear. They would rather spend that time doing something creative.

There's another benefit to a minimalist wardrobe. Because we choose items that are timeless, we don't need to worry about being out of style. We don't wear eccentric styles so there's no need to be concerned about whether an outfit really suits us, if it's the right combination, or how others might judge us. We don't envy expensive clothes, and we aren't embarrassed about wearing cheap clothes. In other words, we stop worrying about how other people see us.

It's easy to be a little nervous when you walk into a stylish store, but take a minute to think about Steve Jobs, the man who always sported the same outfit. Do you think he would have been nervous if he stepped inside a Comme des Garçons store, wondering what people would think about his outfit?

I used to be overly self-conscious in the past. Just walking around town, I would wonder if people thought my outfit was embarrassing, or didn't quite work. I think that by going minimalist in the clothes that I wear, I've become more relaxed about how others may see me.

The real reason it's hard to dine alone at a restaurant

It's hard to dine alone at a restaurant. Take a Korean barbecue place, for example. Don't you get paranoid that the restaurant staff, as well as the other patrons, might be watching you thinking that you have some nerve to do a one-person barbecue as the meat sizzles on the grill in front of you? That you must be lonely eating by yourself? Well, even if they were, they're only thinking that for ten seconds or so, thirty seconds tops. Yet because we are focused completely on ourselves when we're having a solitary barbecue, we tend to think that we're being watched like that during our entire dinner. But put yourself in the place of those around you and you'll see that no one's all that interested in you. As I said earlier, you're the only one who's worried about you.

I don't think it's possible to prove what others may be thinking. Say you approached another patron and said to him, "Hey, you were thinking how lonely I must be to be eating alone, weren't you?" Maybe he'd say no, either to be polite or because it's actually true. Maybe you'd follow up, saying you can prove it because he was staring and laughing at you until a minute ago, but you still won't be able to counter if he says he was just laughing about something else.

Maybe he was in fact thinking about what a lonely diner you are. Maybe he wasn't. It's impossible to prove either way. It's useless being hung up over something that you can't prove. It's even more of a lost cause if you're unable to do as you like because you're worried about how others might see you. If you want to have a private barbecue dinner, well, why not just go for it? No one's as concerned about you as you may think. Everyone's busy and wrapped up with their own lives.

Keeping up appearances only holds us back

There was a time when I wasn't quite comfortable with e-books. Print books are wonderful—it's quick and easy to turn the pages, they have that analog sense of warmth, and the intricate binding work is fun and easy on the eyes.

I think the real reason why e-books gave me a sense of unease, though, was not because they lack the appeal of paper as much as the fact that they simply can't be stacked up after reading. I owned an enormous number of books that I had thought I liked and collected, only to realize that I just picked them up for the sake of appearance. I wanted people to see them and be impressed by what a person of depth I was and how thirsty I must have been for knowledge.

It's clear now that I wanted to convey to others what a worthy person I was through my books. For that purpose, they absolutely had to be piled up in stacks as I finished reading them.

Anyone who sees a pile of books will think that you've read a lot. I felt uneasy about e-books because it would only look like I'd read a single book regardless of how many thousands of works I'd gone through.

There were many books I had left sitting around unread for years. I had told myself I would read them "one of these days." But I realize now that they were mainly there to keep up my appearance as an intellectual.

Now that I've parted with those unread stacks, I've been able to concentrate on the one book that truly interests me at the moment. As a result, I'm reading more books. Parting with my old books has spurred my interest in new areas. By letting go of the old, I've been able to get hold of the new.

Lessons from an unused camera collection

I like to take pictures. I also like to think I have pretty comprehensive knowledge about photography. There had been a time when I used my kitchen as a darkroom for color negatives. I collected beautiful antique cameras and visited auctions to buy one rare camera after another. I displayed them in my apartment, and I never once actually loaded them with film.

I never used them. They were just a part of the décor. They were there so I could tell people I had a lot of cameras, so I could appear to be a camera enthusiast with an artistic streak.

I've since sold all my cameras. I used an auctioning agent and parted with everything at once, including my moisture-proof storage cabinet. By going ahead and parting with all these things that I had clung to for the sake of appearance, I began to worry less about how I looked in the eyes of others. I was able to let go of the useless pride and self-consciousness that plagued me like an extra layer of fat, preventing me from actually pursuing the things that mattered most to me.

My apartment has reached a state where it's no problem to show any part of it to anyone at any time. The same goes for my backpack and my wallet. I'm no longer embarrassed about doing anything. From this point on, I'm simply going to do whatever I feel like doing.

I'm more engaged
with the world around me.

Whatever you do will be insignificant,
but it is very important that you do it.

—attributed to MAHATMA GANDHI

I'm no longer a superintrovert

I now have time. I'm not afraid of how people see me. I easily keep up with housework, which leads to more confidence. This is how the positive cycle of minimalism begins, and what started as a tiny swirl will gradually become a bigger circle. Because of this cycle, there is no longer anything that prevents me from trying something.

Here are just a few of the challenges I've tackled since becoming a minimalist that wouldn't have been possible for the old me:

- Tried scuba diving for the first time (I had been thinking about taking it up for years)
- Made Zen meditation a regular habit (I nervously took part in a Zen session held by Ryunosuke Koike)
- Participated in a yoga program at my gym (I used to think that people would laugh at how stiff my body was)
- Started contacting people I want to meet (people are willing to see me, even celebrities!)
- Participated in face-to-face meetings with minimalists from all over Japan (these are always a lot of fun!)
- Became friends with people I met through the Internet (I now have friends I can go and see everywhere in the country!)

- Started a website (I used to think that people who self-promote were too self-obsessed)
- Joined Twitter (I used to think that people who used Twitter were . . . well, it might be best to leave that out)
- Finally moved for the first time in a decade (it took thirty minutes but it shouldn't take more than twenty minutes next time)
- Declared my love to a girl I thought was beyond my reach and started going out with her (the old me never would have had the guts to do this)
- Wrote a book, of course (the old me would have said forget it, you're only going to embarrass yourself)

The girl I began to date eventually dumped me, but I've been nursing my wounds by telling myself that it was because I still haven't fully grasped the true lessons of minimalism. I realize now I was always too busy worrying about how she would see me.

Going forward, I'm going to focus on studying English. I'm also planning to enjoy the outdoors. I'd like to try my hand at surfing and maybe a little mountain climbing, and I've got my heart set on getting a motorcycle license as well. What's happened to the introvert that I used to be? Was I kidnapped by aliens? Did they plant a chip in me when I wasn't looking?

Nothing that complicated (or exciting), of course. All I did was say goodbye to my things.

I'd rather regret something I've done than something I wish I had done

The regret we experience for not doing something leaves a much stronger impression on us than the regret we may have for doing something. In psychology, this is called the Zeigarnik effect, which says that people remember things that they once pursued and left incomplete more than they do the things that they had completed.

For example, I'm sure most of us regret not telling someone we loved them, and those feelings are likely to remain with us forever. Knowing that we were too scared to try leaves us with an even bigger regret than the fact that we didn't do it. The lesson is clear: if there's something you want to do, now's the time to do it, whether it ends in success or failure.

That's why I wrote this book. I may regret it later. But I'm sure I would have regretted not doing it more. Overall, taking action leads to happiness.

Minimalists can take risks

If you want to keep up the standard of living that you've built over the years and not let go of the items that you've accumulated, you have to preserve the status quo, and that means no changes and no risks. Whether or not you love your job, you have to keep it to maintain your quality of life and to hang on to all your possessions. It's often said that you have to endure your job to "put food on the table" or "enjoy the nicer things in life." But wait. Most of those "nicer things," and the money we need for them, are just for show. We're driven by pride rather than need.

Have less, be free, and you'll be able to go anywhere, whenever you want. You won't be worried about how others see you so you'll be able to take on new challenges without being afraid of failure. Our minimum living costs will decrease when we part with our possessions, which means we'll have more freedom to choose our jobs.

I used to be stuck, comparing the pros and cons of taking every action. I spent all my time looking for the most efficient, and safest, method to reach a goal, but I never did anything. Now I take action. I'm no longer worried about preserving some status quo. Seriously, minimalists have no possessions that they are scared to lose. That gives them the optimism and courage to take risks.

Experiences can't be taken from you

Perhaps the most important reason for getting out there and engaging with the world is that the experiences you gain through your actions can never be taken away from you. Unlike our material possessions, our experiences are inside ourselves, and we can take them with us any place we go. No matter what may happen to us, the experiences are ours to keep.

I can focus better.
I can concentrate on being me.

*I'm as proud of what we don't do
as I am of what we do.*

—STEVE JOBS

The silent to-do list

When we let go of our possessions, our ability to concentrate improves. Why might this be?

Things don't just sit there. They send us silent messages. And the more the item has been neglected, the stronger its message will be.

Maybe there's an English textbook that I gave up on before I even got halfway through it. It might be looking at me now and saying something like *You look bored. Why don't you try to study me again?*

Or there's a dead lightbulb that has yet to be replaced: *Don't tell me you forgot to buy my replacement yet again! Why can't you do something so simple?*

Or a stack of dirty dishes: *Here we go again. I can never count on you.*

We even get messages from items we use on a daily basis. Imagine what your TV might be saying to you: *Uh, you have a bunch of recordings that you haven't watched yet. Oh, and maybe it's about time you gave me a light dusting.*

And your laptop: *It sure would be nice to have a printer as a friend . . . oh well, nevermind.*

And there's the body soap in the bathroom: *Excuse me, I'm running out!*

As to the bedsheets: *I know you're busy, but would you mind giving me a wash one of these days soon?*

All of our possessions want to be cared for, and they tell us that every time we look at them. They begin to form lines in our head, waiting their turn for us to really look at them and listen to what they have to say.

This line of things gets longer and longer as we acquire more material possessions. I call that list the "silent to-do list." Of course our possessions aren't going to literally tell us to do this and that. Unlike our real-life to-do lists, there aren't any bosses or clients to harass us until we get it done. But when left unattended, it'll grow into a huge to-do list.

It's only natural that when a person—a piece of fifty-thousand-year-old hardware—is told to do too many things at once, they're going to lock up and freeze. I suspect that when we're feeling lazy or unmotivated, it's either because our to-do list is too long or we're surrounded by so many menial tasks that we can't get around to doing what's important.

Giving our important things the space to be important

People often say that a person who has a messy desk isn't very productive, and I think the silent to-do list is the reason why. When a desk is cluttered with unorganized business cards, papers that need to be filed, and reference materials that need to be thrown away, it's essentially a huge silent to-do-list pile that saps our concentration. It'll take forever to find things in that pile, and while we're searching through the clutter for the real to-do list that we need to focus on, we lose track of our priorities.

At that point, the pile becomes overwhelming, our self-respect plummets, the stress builds up, and we escape to our smartphone or go on the Internet and check out some social media—we're trapped in a vicious circle.

When we have fewer possessions, these silent messages will, quite naturally, become fewer as well. Without the pile, there's less effort required to prioritize these messages, and if we do receive a message or two, we have the capacity to respond right away.

This is why it's easier to concentrate when we have fewer material possessions. And with all those excess silent to-do messages gone, we can focus on the truly important things that remain.

Lionel Messi's minimalism

The only way to focus on the important things is to reduce the things that aren't important. As I mentioned in chapter 1, this is the guiding principle of minimalism. I think the soccer star Lionel Messi is one example of someone who fully grasps this principle.

Messi, who plays for FC Barcelona and will probably go down in history as one of the sport's best players, is known for running short distances in his matches. While professional soccer players in general run about ten kilometers per match on average, Messi's average is eight kilometers. In fact, you often see him walking on the field during a match. There's also data that indicate that he not only jogs—instead of running—to get back into a defensive position, he doesn't often make an all-out effort to run on offense, either.

I think Messi's minimalist style is why he is the top player in the world. He has a clear picture of the crucial moments when he needs to go full force to surpass his opponents. To him, scoring is his top priority. He's reduced everything else to save his energy and focus on what's truly important: those crucial opportunities to score.

Steve Jobs, the perfect minimalist

Steve Jobs was not a minimalist simply because he always wore the same thing and removed excess from his products. Minimalism really did guide almost everything he did.

The first thing that Jobs is said to have done after making his comeback to Apple was to donate old documents and machines that were almost covered by cobwebs to a museum. He started out by parting with material objects. He wanted to focus on producing products that would change the world, so he got rid of everything else that wasn't important.

He reduced the number of people who took part in company meetings. He would see someone who he didn't think was needed for a meeting and say to them without hesitation, "Thanks, but you don't have to take part in this meeting." He liked to make decisions with the minimum number of talented people.

I've heard that Apple respected ideas more than it did processes, which follows the same principle. In many companies, a designer could come up with a fantastic concept but it would eventually be watered down as it went through marketing, advertising, sales, and so on. Jobs despised such processes and did away with them. He believed that the more signatures you need to approve a product, the more boring the idea is going to become, and the more time it's going to take for it to become a finished product.

In almost everything he did, Jobs started not by prioritizing what he would do but rather by focusing first on what not to do. In that sense, he really was the perfect minimalist. He dedicated himself to getting rid of things.

The happiness of *flow*

Psychologist Mihaly Csikszentmihalyi studied a state of happiness, triggered by concentration, that he called *flow*. When people are completely involved in something, they're not only able to forget their problems, they actually lose track of the passing of time. With further concentration, even the notion of ego or self can disappear. They begin to feel a sense of contentment and the joy of living.

The key to flow is the sense of contentment with the passing of time. The consumption of an engrossing movie or TV series may mask the passing of time, but it doesn't lead to a state of flow.

Csikszentmihalyi's example is the performance of music, but really if you've ever been so immersed in doing something complicated that you've forgotten everything else, you've probably been in a state of flow.

Flow isn't something that everyone can discover. But you'll know with certainty when you find it because you'll be able to immerse yourself into a deeper state of concentration than you've experienced before. That level of concentration is rarely possible until we've reduced all distractions and unnecessary things. Once we have, we open up the possibility of flow, and we can go on to find more happiness.

Information minimalism

Human beings are fifty-thousand-year-old pieces of hardware. Neither our brains nor our bodies have significantly evolved since fifty thousand years ago. Even though recent generations have grown up with digital technology and web connectivity, it doesn't mean our brains suddenly have more storage space or better memory. If we overload our brains, we'll freeze up just like old computers.

Reduce your possessions and you'll receive fewer messages from them. Less memory will be required for dealing with those items and your brain will be able to function more comfortably. The same thing can be said for information. In this section, I'd like to talk about reducing the amount of information that we obtain—what I call "information minimalism."

Folding up your antenna

You may have heard the term "junk information" before. We might see something on the web that seems to grab our attention at first, only to later realize that there hadn't been much meaning to it—if we haven't already forgotten all about it, that is. Consuming too much junk information will lead to a state of "information metabolic syndrome." Tests have shown that people flooded with excess amounts of information performed worse on brain tests than when they smoked marijuana.

The issue now is not how much of that excess information we can obtain, but instead how we can distance ourselves from those flows and decrease the amount of useless information that we take in.

The amount of information available today continues to grow at an explosive rate. If you own a smartphone, then you've probably checked your e-mail before even realizing it, and then found yourself clicking on various links or maybe playing games, for hours on end. Rather than broadening the reach of your antenna, the more important thing to do is to fold it up and decrease the amount of information that you absorb.

One key way to fold up your antenna is to just reduce the opportunities you have to access information. We often hear about exhaustion from excessive dependence on social media, or stress from always being connected with others. Tomohiko Yoneda's *Digital detox no susume* (Digital Detox Recommendations) offers interesting examples of ways to disconnect. There's a hotel with a digital detox plan, where you hand over your smartphone and laptop at check-in. There are smartphone-free bars where you can just focus on having conversations with people over drinks. Volkswagen has banned e-mail communication among employees late at night and early in the morning, and Daimler has introduced a system where e-mails sent to employees during their vacations are automatically deleted. These companies are trying to reduce information overload for the sake of people's personal lives.

Meditation, Zen, and yoga

Many minimalists meditate and practice Zen or yoga, which is quite natural when you think about it. When you decrease the number of material possessions that you have, you become less distracted by your surroundings and your awareness naturally shifts inward.

I used to have a bias against meditation—it had this New Age, sketchy feel. But one day, I had the opportunity to take part in a Zen session with the monk Ryunosuke Koike. It was amazing. Meditation became a habit.

Various thoughts go through your mind when you meditate. You focus on those thoughts and concentrate on simply breathing. Your power of concentration starts to improve, making it second nature, even when you aren't meditating. You learn to grasp and direct your train of thought. For me, Zen and meditation have improved my state of mind so much it's as if I were reinstalling my personal operating system. Google and Facebook are also pretty heavily into Zen and meditation. Google holds meditation workshops, and I hear they even created labyrinths for walking meditation in their offices.

It's easy to drown in the flood of information around us. Making a little time for inner reflection like meditation, Zen, and yoga can help a lot.

Using minimalism to concentrate on being yourself

Since I became a minimalist, I think the haze that had always enveloped my muddled senses has been slowly clearing up.

I was like an unfocused college student. I would read and watch all sorts of things, as long as they had already received high acclaim. I was studying great people and great works, but I wasn't really making my own choices; I was just consuming information haphazardly. All that, I think, has started to change.

Having minimized my material possessions, I've also started to minimize the information I take in. I no longer follow useless news, gossip, or random stand-up comedy. I don't try to fill my conversations with things that other people have made or done. Instead of focusing on the voices of others, I focus on and believe in the voice that's coming from me. What I often feel now is that I'm "returning" to myself.

I used to feel that so many great things had already been produced in the world that there was nothing I could add. I was so worried about what other people would think that I developed an oversized fear of making mistakes. If I came up with a great idea, I'd reject it because it came from me.

This is what I imagine. There used to be another "me" who lived inside me. He had the same size, shape, and form as my usual "self." But the more concerned I became about the outside world, the smaller the inside me got. He was so battered that he could barely get back on his feet. But I now feel as though that little old me has finally gotten up. Minimalism has given me the focus to revive my inner me.

I save money and I care more
about the environment.

*To be smart enough to get all that money
you must be dull enough to want it.*

—GILBERT KEITH CHESTERTON

Minimalism's minimal costs

Minimalism is a very effective way to cut down on costs. We save money in various ways when we become minimalists, and in some cases we may even gain money.

1. Fewer material possessions means we don't need a big house to live in, which means a lot less spent on housing.
2. Selling everything we've collected to date will bring in some money.
3. We're more selective when we buy something, which means less money wasted on frivolous purchases.
4. We're satisfied with the things that we already have, which will lead to less desire for other possessions going forward.
5. Minimalism reduces stress, which helps us eliminate the food and drink costs that had previously existed just for stress relief.
6. We won't be as worried about how others see us as we were before. As a result, we won't need to spend more than what's truly necessary for weddings, child care, funerals, and other events.
7. Using minimalism at work will likely lead to more efficiency and a higher income.

Will minimalism lead to a collapse of the economy?

Some people might worry about the potential risks to the economy if more and more people turn to minimalism. But minimalism isn't quite that simple. There are of course minimalists who don't care about possessions, but there are also those who love material objects. Take a dinner plate, for example. The focus for one person might be cost-effectiveness—they may be perfectly happy with dinnerware from a dollar store—while the next person might want to use an exquisite item created by a master craftsman.

I'm one of those minimalists who love things. I take one look at a magazine and I still enjoy seeing all the things that I'd like to get. The only thing that's changed is that I no longer buy things *just* because I want them. I've certainly become more careful about how I spend my money, but I do still spend money in the end.

For example, I've started spending money more on experiences and people than on material objects. I'd like to travel and spend more time in contact with nature. I spend money on transportation to see the people who I want to see. I help crowdfund projects that I think are interesting. If I see people looking for new ways to live, I'll contribute to them directly.

Minimalism is very effective for cutting down on costs, but it isn't limited to just that. We can change the way we use money—we can direct it away from things that are just for show, and invest instead in experiences, people, or new initiatives. We can spend our money where it's really important.

Minimizing our waste

After discarding a lot of my possessions, I've found myself wanting to minimize the amount of waste I create going forward. I used to have doubts about LOHAS (lifestyles of health and sustainability) and eco-activities, but minimalism has changed my outlook. I always used to buy two-liter bottles of water, but with this niggling sense of wastefulness, I switched to using a Brita water filtration system. I've tried using a solar lantern at night that can be charged in the sun during the day. Living with fewer possessions, I have little in the way of electric appliances and my electricity bills have gone down. Now I want to keep my gas and water bills minimal as well. When you live a life surrounded only by the things that are really necessary, you tend to develop a desire to reduce everything else that isn't essential as well—like garbage and energy—and live simply in a compact way.

The resources that we have will eventually be depleted. Discussions about the earth's resources generally mention another century or so of productive mining years. We won't be around three or four generations from now, but that doesn't mean that we shouldn't worry about the future. I've heard about a Native American teaching that says when something needs to be decided, they look seven generations ahead, which seems to make much more sense.

When you become a minimalist, the energy you use will also become minimal. You won't need to try to live in an eco-friendly way—it'll come naturally. By minimizing your possessions and settling into a focused, simple life, you'll find that the weight on your shoulders has become lighter and you're living in a way that's gentler on the environment. And you know what? It gives you a pretty good feeling.

I'm healthier and safer.

A table, a chair, a bowl of fruit and a violin;
what else does a man need to be happy?

—ALBERT EINSTEIN

Minimalists are slim

I've met a lot of minimalists but none of them (at least so far) have been overweight. I wonder why? I've read in a lot of books on de-cluttering that weight loss is an added bonus that results from discarding your extra things. Since I became a minimalist, I've lost about ten kilos (about twenty-two pounds) myself. Many others have described this effect by observing that when the things that have been stuck around you begin to move, your *chi*—the life force that flows through everything—will flow better and you will also slim down. I think there are other, more specific, things happening as well.

I think there are several reasons why you might lose weight when you part with your possessions. We often gain weight because we're eating more than our bodies need. Maybe we're eating too much because it relieves stress. We can forget about our problems while we're eating. The same can certainly be said for drinking.

When you say goodbye to your things, you'll have less stress because there aren't all those things around that soak up your energy. By not comparing yourself with others, you'll relieve even more stress. You'll have fewer reasons to turn to food and drink.

Gaining a clear awareness
of our desire to eat

When you reduce your possessions to a minimum, you have a clearer and better awareness of your desires. What are the things that are necessary and what are the things that you simply want? The line between these categories becomes clear, and it doesn't apply only to objects. The same goes for our desire to eat. You can see what amounts of food are really necessary and the result is that you don't eat more than you need to. Owning only the things that you need will hone your sense that *This is enough for me*, and you can be satisfied without having to eat huge amounts of food.

There's a diet method in Japan called the *chokomaka* (restless) diet, which literally means moving around in a restless, continuous way, rummaging around here and there to use up calories. Maybe it's because my apartment's gotten more spacious and I enjoy doing housework that these little steps lead to weight loss. I often like to pretend I'm a pitcher and practice pitching moves in my roomy, furniture-free apartment.

The reduction in the things that I carry around with me has also made me more active, and I walk a lot more than I used to. It may sound too simple to be true, but I really think you can lose weight when you do away with your possessions. I used to be overweight. But I don't think I'll ever be that way again.

The danger of things in a natural disaster

I've heard it said that some homeless people actually worry about homeowners. They feel that although they wouldn't be seriously hurt in the event of an earthquake, it would be devastating to anyone in a home. A shelter made of cardboard boxes can collapse in an earthquake but it won't cause much more damage than a bump on the head. A house that collapses will often take the lives of its residents with it. The bigger they are, the harder they fall.

A big earthquake occurred in Tokyo in May 2014. It had been a while since such an event had last occurred. It measured four on the Japanese seismic scale of zero to seven. In the past, I used to jump into my futon and brace myself for objects to come flying at me—my computer, the clothes that were hanging around in my apartment, and a bunch of other things—but when this earthquake occurred, I had gotten rid of a lot of my possessions so there wasn't much that I had to do. The sense of security that I felt at the time was a little disorienting.

With fewer possessions, there are fewer things that will come flying at me. At the time of the Great East Japan Earthquake in 2011, I had a huge bookcase in my hallway, and a lot of books went crashing to the floor. The damage in the Tokyo area was mild from that event, but what if that big earthquake had hit Tokyo directly? My bookcase itself probably would have crashed to the floor and it might have prevented me from getting out of my apartment. My big cameras could have hit my head. My favorite possessions—all those books and cameras—could have killed me.

I think we also need to remember that the tsunami that hit northern Japan during the Great East Japan Earthquake swallowed up family albums and all sorts of important memorabilia. By saving our precious memories digitally, not only on our hard drives but with data backup online through Dropbox or Google Drive, we won't end up losing those important moments in the event of a huge disaster.

And of course Japan isn't unique when it comes to natural disasters. Maybe you live in an area with frequent tornadoes, hurricanes, or even forest fires. In all these cases, your things can suddenly become dangerous.

Isn't it a good idea to reduce the things you own? The less you have, the less you're likely to have destroyed in a disaster, and the less you'll have to do to prepare for a disaster.

We don't even need forty seconds to get ready

No matter what happens, I can always move around as long as I'm physically safe. Moving into my new apartment took less than half an hour, and I no longer have anything truly important at home. They're all things that I can buy again anywhere, and there are no keepsakes that I'll miss if they're lost.

In Hayao Miyazaki's film *Castle in the Sky*, the pirate Dola told Pazu to be prepared in forty seconds. In Steven Spielberg's

War of the Worlds, Tom Cruise shouted at the kids to get ready in sixty seconds so they could escape an attack by aliens. I don't need that much time. I always have my valuables and a minimal change of clothing in a carry-on case that I can take aboard aircraft. I can get out of bed, pull out my carry-on case, get ready, and be out the door within twenty seconds.

With fewer possessions, there will be less risk of damage during a natural disaster. There will be fewer risks in any type of situation, and you can move around quickly regardless of what may happen. That feeling of security can energize us, and reduce our stress levels even further.

My interpersonal relationships
are deeper.

*The value of a man should be seen in what he gives
and not in what he is able to receive.*

—ALBERT EINSTEIN

Don't look at people as objects

I have a favorite book series by the Arbinger Institute that talks about how you can step out of your own little box. Put simply, it explains how personal relationships get disturbed and how they can be put back on track.

There's one example that often comes up. Say there's a working couple that's always busy. The husband sees a big load of laundry that has been washed and he thinks about putting it away so his wife doesn't have to deal with it. But then he changes his mind and decides not to do it. This momentary rejection of his thought is called self-betrayal. He's betrayed the feeling of consideration that came up in that moment.

The husband then starts to think that he's busier than his wife is. He's more tired than she is. The laundry isn't something that he's responsible for. He's done it more often than she has. Then his thoughts are turned toward his wife: she's sloppy, she never thanks him for taking care of the clothes, and she's no good as a wife. Because he betrayed his initial thought of consideration, he started to justify his nonaction, which then led to ill feelings toward the woman he loves.

Meanwhile, the wife will see the laundered clothes and decide to put them away, but not before noticing and then complaining that her husband hasn't done anything about them . . . and the cycle will continue. Both parties will justify their own actions and blame the other, which will only lead to more tension in their relationship.

The book series is really wonderful and I highly recommend it. One of its conclusions is that we shouldn't look at people as objects. It's easy for us to consider our family members, coworkers, and neighbors as fixed objects. Our routine conversations with them can make them seem like sophisticated robots or interactive things. And once we start to see them as things, we'll end up treating them without much consideration.

When this happens, our interpersonal relationships will become fixed without room for improvement. Deeper relationships are only possible if we see every person as a real human being with the same meaningful desires, concerns, and fears. With more time and less stress, we can stop betraying our urges and take actions for the good of others. We can begin to see people as people instead of objects.

Fewer possessions mean fewer disputes

Consider that load of laundered clothes that became the cause of friction between a married couple. What if they had few clothes to begin with? What if taking care of the laundry was much simpler in the first place?

By doing away with my possessions, I've come to love housework, from doing the laundry to cleaning up in the kitchen. Me, the king of laziness. It's simply because these tasks have become much easier.

I'm thirty-five and single, but I know that I'll continue to love doing the housework as long as I continue to live in a small home and have few possessions. In my wild imagination, I can even see my future wife wiping things down with a rag and thinking, *Hey, that's not fair! There she is again, polishing the house and polishing herself. I wanted to do that!*

The minimalists who I've interviewed have told me that parting with their possessions resulted in fewer arguments in their homes. Ofumi, one of the people I mentioned at the beginning of this book, confirmed that she and her husband get along much better since they said goodbye to all their extra things. Yamasan also shared an interesting story: When her two kids had separate rooms, they often fought over which room they wanted, but that stopped when they were told that they'd be sharing a room. She said her kids actually preferred the shared room and thanked her.

The more material possessions you have, the more energy you need to handle your everyday household chores. You become stressed, then frustrated, and you're likely to want to blame those who aren't eager to help out. You'll be thinking of them as robots that should be doing as much work as you are. Discard your things as much as possible and your relationships will become deeper. There will be fewer things to trigger frustration and friction.

The advantages of a small home

Consider the benefits of a small home. First, it's been said that smaller homes can help prevent crimes. Homes where people can go to their rooms without seeing any of their family members or roommates, or huge houses where residents have no idea what's going on in other wings or on other floors, can be dangerous.

There are also advantages for everyday living. Although there's a strong tradition of giving children their own rooms, I think kids who study in their living room at home are probably less likely to consider other people to be irritating distractions as they grow up.

Numahata, with whom I run a website, says he sometimes has arguments with his wife. He says there's one rule that they never break: they never turn their backs to each other and run into their own room. If you live in a small house, it's often simply not possible to escape to your room. You really have no choice but to try to face the problem and understand each other to find a solution.

A small house may not seem to have advantages, but it actually produces positive effects for interpersonal relationships, and it's less expensive to boot. By parting with your material possessions, you open yourself up to the possibility of a small home and all its advantages.

My "family + TV" theory

When you get together with relatives you haven't seen in a while, it can sometimes be hard to find things to talk about. This is when television becomes quite handy. You turn on the TV and quickly find something that you can talk about. I call this my "family + TV" theory.

Unfortunately, I can't use this theory in my apartment. I don't have a TV—the only things I do have are a bedroom and a living room. There's nothing spectacular about the floor plan and I barely have anything in the rooms, which might make some guests uncomfortable when they first arrive. They can't look around and comment on the interesting layout or ask me where I bought my couch. I can't turn on the TV to fall back on the family + TV strategy, and I don't have any games that we can play together. All I can do is serve them tea and chat.

Yet tea service is well suited to family visits—the essence of tea is for the person drinking it and the person who's serving it to think about each other. My living room is basically a tearoom. Just like in the tearooms used for Japanese tea ceremonies, the only thing that we can do is to face each other, even if the words don't come smoothly. No one gets angry if there's no TV set or radio in a tea ceremony room. All you can do is to drink your tea and talk about the thoughts that are going through your mind.

The secret to a happy marriage

I lose track of time when I visit the home of a minimalist and chat in a place that's free of clutter. We focus on each other and talk without being distracted by anything. It's the opposite of a scene that I often come across: two people sitting at a table, with one or both of them playing around on their smartphones. I'm not sure if they're playing games or believe that friends on social media are more important than the person they're with, but I think relationships will change for the better if people begin to focus on real people.

I've heard it said that the secret to a happy marriage is to simply talk a lot with your partner. One study showed that happily married couples talked with each other five more hours per week than couples that aren't happy. If people are busy taking care of their possessions, quarreling over them, spending time in separate rooms, or watching a lot of TV, they're naturally going to have less time for conversations.

People are just human beings

I think my self-awareness has changed quite a bit since parting with my possessions. I'm a regular guy who owns very little and walks around in a normal outfit, almost like a duck or a turtle that swims around in a pond just living life.

By thinking of myself as just another human being, my perspective of others has also changed. The jealousy I felt when I saw someone with a lot of money, things, or talent, and the scorn I had for people who had very little—all these feelings have started to disappear.

I can now meet people who own a lot of things or are blessed with enormous talent without feeling embarrassed about myself. I no longer blame people who have very little for not trying hard enough. No one's better because they have or don't have a lot. Rich or poor, famous or ordinary, we're all just human beings who come into contact with one another. My relationships with people have become more genuine since I began to think this way.

I can now see someone simply as another human being without ranking them based on what they have. As a result, I don't think I'll ever again feel embarrassed about myself when I meet someone.

What if you had a hundred friends?

I heard something interesting from a person who often helps me out in my work. He's a wonderful man who has a kind, gentle smile and an appealing personality. He mentioned that when he decides to have a birthday party, a hundred friends show up to celebrate. Everyone brings along a bottle of wine, his favorite drink.

I don't have many friends, and I felt truly envious when I heard this. With so many friends who love you and are eager to celebrate with you, you probably won't ever feel very lonely, and you know that there are always a lot of people you can rely on if you're ever in trouble.

But then again, the man also told me that he's out celebrating someone else's birthday about once every three days. I guess if you have a hundred friends, they'll all want you to celebrate with them too—which means, yeah, you're likely to have one party or another every three days.

What if you had just a few, true friends?

There's a saying that we only truly need three close friends or colleagues. It's true that if you saw each of your three close friends once every weekend, every month would be deeply satisfying. Minimal interpersonal relationships like that can be wonderful. We tend to think that it's better to have lots of friends and connections, but if you have so many friends that you can't be attentive to each person, what's the meaning of building ties in the first place?

Why not try minimizing your superficial relationships so that you can give each of your friends the attention and respect they deserve? In the same way that material objects that are truly necessary for us will always find a way to come back to us, a deep, heartfelt friendship should always be possible to repair.

That said, we should not get carried away with minimizing our relationships. In the film *Into the Wild*, the protagonist Chris McCandless leaves us with words I think are worth living by: "Happiness [is] only real when shared."

The island where people live longest

As McCandless taught us, what's important in life is to have relationships with people with whom happiness can be shared. It's also known that happy people live longer lives. Psychologist Ed Diener has pointed out from his research analysis that people who have a strong sense of happiness live 9.4 years longer on average.

Sardinia, a beautiful Italian island, is where people live the longest lives in the world—two and a half times longer than the global average, with one out of every four thousand residents over the age of a hundred. There's a village in Sardinia where the oldest siblings, as recognized by the Guinness World Records, live. It's a village where most of the residents are related in some way and know one another, where interpersonal relationships are smooth, and daily living is comfortable. Family and relatives live close enough so people can get together whenever they want, and of course there's reliable support from fellow villagers. It's a community filled with love that supports longevity. The villages in Okinawa, Japan, which are also known for their longevity, also have a culture where everyone you meet is considered a brother or sister. Older people keep an eye over the children in the neighborhood, and people nurture trusting relationships and cherish the sense of community.

The happier people are, the longer they'll live. When you look at the people who've been enjoying long lives, there will be barely any exceptions to the fact that fine relationships have been nurtured among them. You don't need to have a hundred friends. There are some people who don't have family. But scores of research results indicate that ties with neighbors and treasured friends are indispensable for happiness.

Mirror neurons and built-in kindness

Mahatma Gandhi, who taught nonpossession, said, "Service which is rendered without joy helps neither the servant nor the served. But all other pleasures and possessions pale into nothingness before service which is rendered in a spirit of joy."

Even if we can't serve others like Gandhi did over the course of his life, it's true that we experience a sense of joy when we do something for another person. We do something for them and they look happy. We see them smile and it makes us smile, and we forget about the trouble we may have gone to. Why does this happen?

Science is beginning to show that doing something for another person might actually lead to happiness. The discovery of mirror neurons is a good example. Don't you feel the pain when you see someone getting hurt? When you watch a person fall? Scientists have hypothesized that mirror neurons are what make us feel like we're experiencing something just by watching the actions being taken by another person.

This might be the reason why we can get totally absorbed in a novel, comic book, a TV drama, or a movie. We feel sad when a lead character experiences sadness, and we're happy when we see a happy ending. We can empathize because of this function.

There are also other systems for us to empathize with others. Suppose you see a scene in a video where a large number of people are frantic to save one child who has been left stranded in the river in a major flood. Just by seeing this scene, you're filled with emotion and might shed a tear. This is not necessarily because you have an unusually kind heart.

The mere act of seeing people helping one another out prompts endorphins—neurotransmitters that bring us joy—to be released in the brain. And it's not just from watching; we can also feel happy by taking action ourselves. For example, we've all experienced that warm feeling when you offer your seat on the train to a senior or to a pregnant woman, or when you see a person drop something on the street and return it to them. That feeling comes from endorphins being released inside us.

In a way, we're basically equipped to empathize with others because we feel happy when we're nice to someone. Because we are social animals that live in packs, we're programmed to share happiness when we do something for another person.

When you reduce the number of things you own, you can devote more time and energy to your interpersonal relationships.

You won't need to depend on your possessions for happiness because we're already equipped with systems that let us feel happy simply by connecting with the people around us.

I can savor the present moment.

*The distinction between the past, present and future
is only a stubbornly persistent illusion.*

—ALBERT EINSTEIN

I don't think about the future

I've said goodbye to a lot of things. Every time I've parted with my possessions, I've continued to ask myself if I need them *now*, not some day in the future. As I've kept on asking myself about the present and erased the concept of *someday*, a strange thing has happened. For some reason, I am no longer able to think about the future. It's as if curtains have been drawn and blocked out all those worries about the future. Even when I try to think about them, I can't. And all I've done is part with my possessions.

Trying to wash dishes that aren't even dirty yet

Things had been completely different before I said goodbye to things. I was always thinking about the uncertainties that the future had in store for me. I'd chosen to work in publishing, a declining industry. I wasn't particularly spectacular as an editor, and the scope of my work wasn't all that great. A major blow to the business would probably mean an immediate loss of employment, and a career change would be tough at the age of thirty-five. I'm not married, I have no kids, and I have no particularly close friends to speak of. The only thing that waits for me in the future is a lonely death. I knew it was negative, but I was always afraid of what lay ahead.

There's a favorite quote of mine from Dale Carnegie's *How to Stop Worrying and Start Living* that really sums up what was wrong with me: "I was trying to wash today's dishes, yesterday's dishes and dishes that weren't even dirty yet." The dishes that need to be washed today are those that were used during the course of a single day. Anyone would collapse in despair if they started thinking about washing the dishes tomorrow, the day after, and every day over the course of a year. They wouldn't even be able to catch up with the dishes that need to be washed today. Future unemployment, marriage, having kids, getting old and getting sick, and dying alone—these were the dishes in my future that weren't even dirty yet.

I learned a lot just by parting with my possessions. I realized if I had something that I might use one day in the future, I could let it go and buy it later when that time came (if it came at all). If I found out after parting with something that I actually needed it, I could just buy it then.

It's true that I might lose my job and it's also true that I might die alone. I've come to realize that I can worry about all that if and when that happens.

Goodbye past things, goodbye old me

In a similar way, I no longer have anything that I used to need in the past. By asking myself if I need something *now*, I've been able to discard the things that used to be important to the old me. I don't have the things I used to believe were a part of me. Now,

I'm just a human being who no longer owns anything that is tied up with my identity.

I used to be a gloomy insular soul, but now I no longer have anything left to prove just how introverted I'd been. What remained after I parted with all these things was the present. By parting with my possessions, I'm no longer stuck with the old me.

I threw away everything I thought would be needed for *some day* in the future, as well as the things I thought I needed in the past. I was left with what truly matters: the present.

You can only experience the *now*

We're the only animals that have the ability to predict the future. But as we discussed in chapter 2, that ability is primitive, effective only for predicting the immediate future. We can decide whether to flee from an enemy in the next five seconds, or which direction we should take to capture our prey. We can imagine how we'd feel immediately after we buy an iPhone. But there isn't a single person in the world who can accurately predict how they'll feel when they look at that iPhone a year from now.

Even if we could predict our futures, consider this: None of us can actually experience that future. Maybe we can try to clearly imagine it, but we'll never experience it the way we experience the present.

No one can experience vividly a past event in the same way that they can experience what they're now feeling, either. The only things that we can recall are edited highlights from our memories. If there's anyone out there who can experience their past through their five senses as they can the present, they might be tempted to sink into the past entirely, reliving their favorite memories forever.

Neither the past nor the future actually exists. There's only an eternal present, and you can only experience the *now*. I think that's what Einstein meant when he said you can't make a distinction between the past, present, and future.

A person who keeps sighing forever

Anyone who believes that they have the ability to experience the future will pay little attention to the present. They'll put up with things and frown if only for the sake of their glorious future. But it's only in the present that they can experience something, which means that those grumpy-looking souls frowning today will probably continue to be sullen no matter what they do.

Or as I like to say, if you're sighing now, you'll probably be sighing forever. If you really want to change something, the only way to do it is to start changing this very moment. There's really no tomorrow, and no next week to look forward to. Once tomorrow comes, it's going to be today. A year from now will be today when the time comes. Everything is in the *now*.

By parting with the things that I'd been keeping for my past and for my future, I now find that I can think only about the present. I'm not going to be afraid of anything that may await me in the future. Without all my old possessions, I have the freedom and mobility to manage, no matter what the future may bring. Isn't it funny the way we say, "What the future may bring"? Even that little saying shows we really believe that the future will actually bring something to us in the present.

I won't be comparing myself with others anymore, and I won't be preparing for far-off futures either. Rich or poor, sad or happy, I'll face it then. All I need to do is experience the *now*.

I feel true gratitude.

There are only two ways to live your life.
One is as though nothing is a miracle.
The other is as though everything is.

—attributed to ALBERT EINSTEIN

The gratitude that comes
from having few possessions

A while back, partway through my minimizing process, I had gotten rid of a lot of things and my apartment had become pretty airy. Lying in bed, I experienced a strange new feeling: for some reason, I was filled with gratitude for all the things that I still had.

It's something I hadn't felt when I was always buying more. Back then, I had always been so preoccupied with what I didn't have that I never even thought about being grateful for what I did have. I had a bed, a desk, and even an air conditioner. I could sleep well, take a shower, prepare my meals, and enjoy my favorite pastimes. It was an apartment where I could relax with peace of mind.

Yet all that stuff actually blocked my gratitude. When would I ever have had the time to thank my TV, my games, my old Blu-ray recorder, my home theater, all the remote controls, and everything else? Gratitude becomes possible only when you don't have many possessions. I've even become grateful for having a roof over my head that protects me from the wind and the rain.

Only gratitude can compete with boredom

Gratitude is the only thing that can prevent the cycle of familiarity leading to boredom that I wrote about in chapter 2. Gratitude allows us to see our everyday life with a fresh perspective—we won't continue to take things for granted if we become aware of our appreciation for them. Through gratitude, we can trigger sustainable stimulation, which gives us much more peace than the stimulation that we get by buying something new or increasing our stockpile.

We can accumulate as much as we like, but without gratitude we'll only end up being bored with everything we've obtained. Conversely, we can achieve true contentment with few possessions, just so long as we treat them with gratitude.

The *Five Reflections* chant

There's a Buddhist chant recited before meals called *Gokan no Ge*, or the Five Reflections.

1. Reflect upon how the food has come before you—how the food might have been grown, how it was prepared, and how it was brought to you as your meal.
2. Reflect upon your virtues and conduct. Are you worthy of the meal?
3. Focus only on the meal in front of you without rushing through it and without thinking any other thoughts.
4. Eat not from a gourmet perspective, weighing whether the meal is tasty, but simply to support your life.
5. Eat so you are able to pursue the objectives that you would like to achieve.

It's a powerful chant. Saying the chant before a thousand meals will give you a richer, more satisfying feeling than eating a $500 meal at a restaurant a thousand times.

Steve Jobs is said to have looked in the mirror each morning and asked himself if he would have liked to follow his schedule if it were the last day of his life. He continued to do this for thirty-three years, so he could check whether he was getting off track. The Five Reflections are another way of checking our conduct on a daily basis.

I'm no longer a gourmet foodie. Please don't get me wrong, I still love to eat good food and I value good ingredients. But now, I spend less time searching online for great places to eat. I'm no longer concerned if people don't think of me as a connoisseur of good food. As long as I remember to feel grateful for my food, I can focus on whatever I might be served and appreciate it.

Gratitude is not a method

The feeling of gratitude is powerful. I was probably taught about the importance of gratitude during ethics lessons in elementary school, but it had completely slipped my mind. It seems like I took a great detour before I realized the importance of such a plain and simple word.

I decided to make it a habit to feel gratitude. I made up my mind and told myself that I would remember to feel grateful for everything. I thought I could make gratitude a method.

With that in my mind, I was flabbergasted when I read a book by Mitsuro Sato called *Kamisama tono Oshaberi* (Conversation with God), which explained that you feel true gratitude only when you're happy.

Let's try to imagine a situation where we might want to shout, "I'm happy!" Soaking in a spacious open-air bathtub at a nice inn with a fabulous meal waiting for us? I think this is the type of situation where we would certainly feel happy.

It's easy to focus on your feelings of gratitude if you're at a terrific inn with a beautiful bath, great food, and a wonderful setting. I probably couldn't help but murmur to myself that I'm happy in a situation like that, and there would certainly be a sense of gratitude there.

I realized then that gratitude is not a method. It's a part of happiness—it's happiness itself. Studies in psychology have shown that the more times people have a chance to be grateful, the happier they'll be. That isn't all that surprising when you consider that gratitude is happiness.

Feeling gratitude right now

As we talked about in the last section, we can only experience the present. You can't vividly relive the past, and you can't throw yourself into the future. We can only feel what's happening now, and everything is in the present. What if we were to combine this with an affirmative perspective filled with gratitude?

Let's just try it for a minute. Let's try to appreciate the present. It's now midnight. I'm sitting at a chain restaurant. It's lonely because I'm the only customer here . . . but wait, the place is staying open late just for me. I'm wearing my usual clothes . . . but they're wonderfully comfortable no matter how many times I wear them. The waiter was curt to me . . . but he quickly brought me my meal, and even asked me to enjoy it. The banquette where I'm sitting is boring . . . but I'm grateful that I can sit here for hours without getting sore. The drink station is the same as it always is . . . but I can have as many cups of coffee as I want, and the cups and glasses are always nice and clean. I step out of the restaurant and feel a little jealous of all the couples I pass . . . but I've got many wonderful memories, too.

Or maybe I'm in the middle of a commute. It's my usual route to get to work and I'm pretty much fed up with it. I'm stuck behind someone having trouble with his commuter pass. He probably forgot to add money to it . . . but these passes are really quite amazing. They're a wonderful invention, so convenient, and we can even use them to buy things at the kiosks. Two people are standing talking to each other on one side of the escalator while I try to get by . . . but it's gratifying to see that they've left one side open so others can get through if they're in a hurry. As usual, the train is absolutely packed . . . but wait, I'm grateful that there are a lot of people around. I'm glad I'm not the sole survivor of some doomed world that you might see in an apocalyptic movie. It's so hot today . . . but once I get to the office, the air conditioners and the fans will be working at full blast. The usual work awaits . . . but it's fun and fulfilling if I concentrate. That one person I'm not too crazy about is sure to call with complaints again . . . but I guess it's another chance to build my experience and expertise. The other person's probably tired, too. I wish my subordinates would be more independent . . . but they're quick to help without a word of complaint. I've been working late continuously and am exhausted . . . but I'm not sick. I'm in good health and I can do a lot more.

Wow. It's amazing how much everyday happiness I can feel when I do this. How about you? When we aim for gratitude right now, we become more positive, tolerant, and generous. Above all, we open ourselves up to everyday happiness, and that openness will eventually change reality.

5

"Feeling" happy instead of "becoming" happy

Letting go of what happiness *should* be

Society has embraced a few standard "examples of happiness" that suggest the ways that we should live our lives: Get a stable job, get married, start a family, have two or three kids. Enjoy your grandchildren. That's widely accepted as a happy life, and most of us (at one point or another) believe we'll be happy as long as we're able to achieve those things.

Positive psychology, a branch of psychology aimed at studying satisfaction and fulfillment, reveals a completely different model for happiness. Psychologist Sonja Lyubomirsky says that 50 percent of our happiness is genetically determined, 10 percent by life circumstances and situations, and the remaining 40 percent by our daily actions. "Life circumstances and situations" includes various factors, such as where we live, whether we're rich or poor, healthy or ill, married or divorced, and so forth.

This is surprising—I'd guess that many people might think happiness would be more like 90 percent life circumstances and situations, and maybe around 10 percent genetics. They might believe anyone who wins the lottery today would live happily ever after. Or maybe just as many people feel that 90 percent of happiness is determined genetically and 10 percent comprises their circumstances. In this case, if you're incredibly gorgeous, you'd be able to achieve happiness quite easily.

Genetics determines 50 percent of our happiness

Based on studies conducted on identical twins raised in different environments, there seem to be unique standards of happiness that people have that support the concept that genetics determines 50 percent of our happiness. This doesn't mean that our appearance, intelligence, or coordination determine our happiness—it means that, like our natural body weight, we all have a certain level that our happiness settles at, regardless of the wonderful, or the tragic, events that happen to us.

Fifty percent of our happiness is based on this natural level. From a very early age, we all develop different personalities. For example, some kids are simply quick to smile from the outset. They're just born that way; they're not trying to force it to become happy. These are the people who grow up always feeling positive no matter what they may be faced with. They always brighten the mood around them. Without question, people like that really do exist. But we're not doomed if we're not one of those people. Remember, genetics accounts for only 50 percent of our happiness.

The environment determines only 10 percent of our happiness

Our environment is said to influence our happiness by a mere 10 percent. It's true that our level of happiness improves dramatically if we can secure minimal standards of safety and procure food and a place to sleep. Happiness can be bought with money up to that point. But any improvements in environment after that have little impact on our happiness. Isn't it strange to think that all those standard life goals—our job, income, home, marital status, whether or not we have kids—only play a 10 percent role in the happiness that we experience?

It's because we get used to things. No matter how much or how little money we have, whether we live in a mansion on a tropical island or a cramped one-room shack in the freezing tundra, our environment affects our contentment by only 10 percent.

Various studies have confirmed this phenomenon. When a major event first occurs, it's perceived as a variance, a stimulus. We will be overjoyed if we win the lottery. We may fall into depression if we become seriously ill or lose a loved one. But most of us soon accept our new circumstances and adjust at a surprising speed.

Graduate from a good school, join a good company, get married, have kids, buy a house, save up for retirement, and enjoy grandchildren. That's a model example of happiness. But no matter how much of this example we achieve, we'll eventually get used to each new step on the ladder.

Our actions determine
40 percent of our happiness

Then comes the remaining 40 percent of what makes us happy, the 40 percent that we can change through our actions. I've mentioned a lot of research results on happiness so far. Did you know that the way that people's happiness is assessed in those studies is actually very simple? The subjects are asked directly. One example might be something like "Looking at things in the long run, are you satisfied with your life?" If people feel happy, neurotransmitters will be released from their brain, which can then be measured to assess whether they're happy. But while those substances might be possible to detect during those moments when the measurements are taken, it isn't possible to say whether those results will hold for a long period of time. It isn't possible to continuously take those measurements throughout the course of people's lives. In the test, happiness is something that has to be declared individually.

Happiness depends on how you interpret it. Happiness isn't something outside you; it's within you. Happiness is always in your heart. Many people have said it in different ways, and they're all right. Happiness is basically something that each of us can measure only by declaring our own sense of contentment ourselves. A person might be in a difficult situation that looks rough to others, but if they feel that they're happy, if they're grateful for their conditions, then that person is happy. That's why our actions make up 40 percent of our happiness. Happiness isn't a state that we win by accomplishing certain criteria. Happiness is something that can only be felt in this moment.

You don't "become" happy

A person once said to me that the only thing missing from his life was children. He believed that he would be content when he achieved that objective. Maybe a lot of people feel the same way. Once they achieve some criteria, they will be able to "become" happy.

It's like reaching the summit of a mountain called "Happy Mountain," where you're guaranteed happiness for the rest of your life. Or running a "Happy Marathon," where you cross the finish line and you're awarded a medal called "Happiness." But happiness isn't on a mountaintop or at a finish line. It isn't possible to "become" happy. That's because every achievement can make you happy for a moment, but you'll soon get used to it. It'll become a part of your daily life, something that'll be taken for granted.

Someone who wins the lottery is very fortunate. They will be able to quit their job and not have to worry about their future. They'll be able to try any of life's pleasures without financial concerns.

But they can't accurately imagine how they'll feel a year after they've taken the grand prize, and they'll likely find that most of their starting joy has faded. We get used to changes, even huge ones. How can someone who wants children, who thinks that kids are all that's missing from his life, imagine how he will be feeling three years after he has a child?

You don't "become" happy. Happiness isn't a reward that you receive for following examples that are set. It doesn't come attached to certain life achievements, and it isn't handed to you on a silver platter.

"Feeling" happy instead of "becoming" happy

I think happiness is something that can only be felt, and it's only in the present that you can truly experience it. It's the feeling of delight that you feel from moment to moment. A person who is unhappy now can't plan to feel happiness tomorrow, the day after, or a year from now, because once that time comes, it will simply be another "now" for them to be unhappy in. To look at it the other way around, there's nothing extra we need to feel happy in this very moment. It's possible for us to always feel happy.

Minimalism maximized the 40 percent of happiness I get from my actions

If our environment can only affect our happiness by 10 percent, why spend time accumulating a lot of material possessions? Why not live in a minimalist apartment and free yourself to change your actions, which are 40 percent of your happiness, by saying goodbye to your things?

For me, minimalism was an essential part of my path to happiness. I now live my days feeling greater happiness than I ever have before. I used to be an introvert who didn't smile or talk very much. People used to say they had no idea what I was thinking, as if I were some sort of robot. But that robot is slowly starting to change.

Because I don't own very much, I have the luxury of time. I can enjoy the simplicity of my daily life without feeling stressed or overwhelmed. That useless pride has disappeared, and since I'm not self-conscious about appearances, I've been able to take the bold step of writing this book.

I have better concentration and I am finally focusing on the work that I've always wanted to do. I'm more perceptive of the here and now. I don't relive past traumas or worry about my uncertain future.

More than anything, though, the biggest change in my behavior since I said goodbye to my things has been the rise of a new sense of everyday gratitude. I am truly moved by my experiences in the present moment, and I find myself walking through life grateful for the friends I have and for those few things I've kept.

Minimalism isn't an objective. It's a method. There are many important lessons that I've learned through minimalism. But if you've already learned these lessons and more, you don't need to become a minimalist. Even I have the freedom to start buying

254 | GOODBYE, THINGS

more things, as long as I continue to cherish the important lessons minimalism has taught me.

Minimal & ism, the website that I run with Numahata, was named with the idea that by reducing our things to a minimal state, we can discover what's really important to us. While following my minimalist path, I think I've discovered what's most important: it's the people around me.

It's not just family and friends, or people who are beautiful, talented, or whose opinions match mine. It includes every person I meet today.

What's important in my life? It's the person who's sitting or standing in front of me right now.

Afterword and maximum thanks

I've become an expert at feeling gratitude, so this is going to be a bit long. I'd like to start by saying that I first came across the term "minimalist" in an article by Naoki Numahata, with whom I now run the Minimal & ism website. The first day I met him, we had an impassioned discussion about minimalism, and it seems like our plans for the website were hatched in that instant. I never believed I was the type of person who had something to offer to others, but I fell in love with writing the blog, which led to the writing of this book. I'm very happy to have made precious friends through minimalism.

I'd also like to thank my employer, Wani Books. They were gracious and supportive when I said—me, an editor—that I wanted to write a book. Everyone must have wondered if I had gone crazy or had only a few months to live, or something. I felt the same way at the time. Had Wani been a bigger company, I probably wouldn't have had the nerve to say anything about my wish.

I extend my heartfelt gratitude to Mr. Yokouchi, the president of our company; Ms. Aoyagi, who heads editorial and so generously supported my unusual project; and my boss Ms. Ichiboji, editor of the photo collection editorial department. I'd like to thank everyone in editorial for pitching in while I was lost in thought about this book for the whole year.

"What's so fun about living in an apartment like this?" Mr. Sakurai, head of our sales department, once asked. I'm really glad that we were able to have such active conversations. Let's go out and sell the book now!

To Mr. Otsuka, the person I kept going back to asking for quote after quote after quote, and everyone in administration: Thank you so much. I hope this book will be something that'll keep everyone in public relations busy. And to the people in the digital business department, I look forward to releasing this in digital format, too. To the people in finance, I'll try not to be late with my invoices for this book. Many thanks also to the people in general administration. And to everyone else in our other departments, thank you for your warm words of encouragement. I was happy to hear you say that you were looking forward to publication.

As an editor who usually works behind the scenes, I'm well aware that a book is delivered to our readers after a lot of hard work by many people. Those at Toppan Printing who printed this book, everyone at National Bookbinding who put this work together, those of you at ALEX Corporation who handled the desktop publishing, the people at Tokyo Shuppan Service Center who were responsible for the proofreading, and the people at

Taiyo Shoji for always transporting our heavy loads of books—thank you all very much. And last but not least, many thanks to the people who serve as our agents and those of you at the wonderful bookstores. I hope you'll continue to offer this book to our readers.

I'd also like to thank Steve Jobs and Apple. It's because of the iPhone and MacBook Air, two truly minimalist products that Mr. Jobs introduced to the world, that I've been able to say goodbye to so many of my material possessions, while also being able to write at any location. It's thanks to Microsoft Word that I was able to write this. I was able to organize my outline thanks to the Tree2 app. Dropbox made it possible to store the material securely. Thanks to the development of various technologies, it's been possible to do this without the need for extra equipment.

I'd also like to mention my gratitude to Jonathan's in Meguro for letting me write most of this work at their restaurant and to the Jonathan's in Fudomae, for letting me write the rest of it at *their* restaurant. I'm sorry for staying at your establishments for so many hours on end. Half of the reason why I chose to move to Fudomae was because of your restaurant. Thank you also to the Tokyo Metropolitan Library, a library with a wonderful garden where I went every day while writing. I was often inspired by the ducks and turtles that swim leisurely in your pond.

To the many minimalists I've had a chance to meet: There were many occasions when I wondered if the changes I've mentioned in this book were things that had happened to me alone. I was happy to meet with every single one of you, so kind, generous, and radiant. I got the impression that by reducing your material possessions, all of you had experienced positive changes in your life and were moving forward. To the minimalists with whom I met for the writing of this book: While the contents here are my personal views, I was immensely stimulated by every one of you. I think of all of you as my friends, and I look forward to seeing you again. Hiji, my participation in the "Minimalist Kyoto Off-Kai" event that you hosted proved to be the first major step that I took. That meeting helped me to change.

To all the minimalists with whom I haven't had a chance to meet but who have helped with the publicity: I believe that the spread of minimalism will help more people become happy and free. Thank you.

The designer Keito Kuwayama. It's thanks to Mr. Kuwayama's God-like swiftness that we managed to work things out in spite of our tight schedule. You work so quickly that I couldn't help taking a step back in wonder—I'm still amazed. Thank you so much for creating a terrific design so incredibly fast.

Shunsuke Murakami, the editor for this book. I never thought there'd be an editor for an editor. I'm really glad I didn't have to do everything by myself. If I had, I probably would have fled somewhere by now. There were often times while I was writing this that I wondered if everything was just a figment of my imagination and nothing would be conveyed to anyone. Those were the times when I remembered Mr. Murakami offering words of support and telling me that what I wrote was interesting. I was also elated by the amount of attention that you gave the work as an editor. I'm sorry I was late with the manuscript. Thank you so much.

Thanks also to all my friends and family who helped advertise this book. Please tell me what you think of it; there's no need to hold back. There's one thing that I must apologize for: I've let go of everything that you've given me. I really am sorry about that. I took pictures of everything, remembering the joy I felt when you gave them to me, and I said goodbye to them with feelings of gratitude. I was able to feel tremendous happiness when I first received them from you and again when I let them go. Thank you so much.

And to all my readers. Thank you for reading this book. I've shared with you all the thoughts I had as I reduced my material possessions. I hope there might be something, even just a short phrase, that stays with you. I'm sure there are many mistakes in here, which I am fully responsible for, and would appreciate it if you would kindly point them out.

Last, to my late father and my dear, healthy mother: If there's anything in the book that gives people a sense of freedom, I think it's the result of your belief not to force your children to do anything and to let them be independent. You allowed me to think for myself. Thank you both from the bottom of my heart.

I would now like to wrap this up with a favorite quote of mine. It's from a poem that was written by the poet Rūmī.

But I will now close my mouth, hoping that you will open yours.

Recap: 55 tips to help you say goodbye to your things

1. Discard the preconception that you can't discard your things.
2. Discarding something takes skill.
3. When you discard something, you gain more than you lose.
4. Ask yourself why you can't part with your things.
5. Minimizing is difficult, but it's not impossible.
6. There are limits to the capacity of your brain, your energy, and your time.
7. Discard something right now.
8. There isn't a single item you'll regret throwing away.
9. Start with things that are clearly junk.
10. Minimize anything you have in multiples.
11. Get rid of it if you haven't used it in a year.
12. Discard it if you have it for the sake of appearance.
13. Differentiate between things you want and things you need.
14. Take photos of the items that are tough to part with.
15. It's easier to revisit your memories once you go digital.
16. Our things are like roommates, except we pay their rent.
17. Organizing is not minimizing.
18. Tackle the nest (storage) before the pest (clutter).
19. Leave your "unused" space empty.
20. Let go of the idea of "someday."
21. Say goodbye to who you used to be.
22. Discard the things you have already forgotten about.

23. Don't get creative when you're trying to discard things.

24. Let go of the idea of getting your money's worth.

25. There's no need to stock up.

26. Feeling the spark of joy will help you focus.

27. Auction services are a quick way to part with your possessions.

28. Use auctions to take one last look at your things.

29. Use a pickup service to get rid of your possessions.

30. Don't get hung up on the prices that you initially paid.

31. Think of stores as your personal warehouses.

32. The city is our personal floor plan.

33. Discard any possessions that you can't discuss with passion.

34. If you lost it, would you buy it again?

35. If you can't remember how many presents you've given, don't worry about the gifts you've gotten.

36. Try to imagine what the person who passed away would have wanted.

37. Discarding memorabilia is not the same as discarding memories.

38. Our biggest items trigger chain reactions.

39. Our homes aren't museums; they don't need collections.

40. Be social; be a borrower.

41. Rent what can be rented.

42. Social media can boost your minimizing motivation.

43. What if you started from scratch?

44. Say "see you later" before you say goodbye.

45. Discard anything that creates visual noise.

46. One in, one out.

47. Avoid the Concorde fallacy.

48. Be quick to admit mistakes. They help you grow.

49. Think of buying as renting.

50. Don't buy it because it's cheap. Don't take it because it's free.

51. If it's not a "hell, yes!" it's a "no."

52. The things we really need will always find their way back to us.

53. Keep the gratitude.

54. Discarding things can be wasteful. But the guilt that keeps you from minimizing is the true waste.

55. The things we say goodbye to are the things we'll remember forever.

Recap: 15 more tips for the next stage of your minimalist journey

1. Fewer things does not mean less satisfaction.

2. Find your unique uniform.

3. We find our originality when we own less.

4. Discard it if you've thought about doing so five times.

5. If you've developed your minimalist skills, you can skip the "see you later" stage.

6. A little inconvenience can make us happier.

7. Discard it even if it sparks joy.

8. Minimalism is freedom—the sooner you experience it, the better.

9. Discarding things may leave you with less, but it will never make you a lesser person.

10. Question the conventional ways you're expected to use things.

11. Don't think. Discard!

12. Minimalism is not a competition. Don't boast about how little you have. Don't judge someone who has more than you.

13. The desire to discard and the desire to possess are flip sides of the same coin.

14. Find your own minimalism.

15. Minimalism is a method and a beginning.